man
and his
environment:
climate

man
and his
environment
series:

edited by
John Bardach,
(*The University of Hawaii*)
Marston Bates,
and Stanley Cain
(*The University of Michigan*)

man
and his
environment:
climate

DAVID M. GATES

The University of Michigan

Harper & Row, Publishers
New York
Evanston
San Francisco
London

contents

editors' introduction

The books of the Harper & Row series being published under the general title of *Man and His Environment* are designed to help us understand the world about us, our dependence on it, and what we are doing to it, both good and bad.

From the personal point of view, it has been said that the environment is everything else but me. It is the sky over our heads and the earth beneath our feet. It is other people and any living animal or plant with which we have any connections. It includes what the senses of sight, hearing, taste, smell, and touch tell us about nature. Also, the environment is home, the cities and towns we have built. It includes the landscape that is altered by raising food, feed, and fiber; by the extraction of minerals; by building homes, schools, churches, places of business, and factories, and by building facilities for travel and transport, for the generation of energy, and for communication. The environment includes not only the natural and man-made things about us but also physical and cultural conditions and processes.

All these elements of the environment can be studied, thought about, and worked with individually, but this analytic approach is inadequate for the understanding of the total environment, and it leads to difficulties when we overlook or neglect the consequences of single-purpose actions. This is because the elements of the environment do not occur singly in nature or in culture, but in complex interacting systems. For example, soil is not just decomposed rock. It includes air and water, hundreds of organic and inorganic compounds, and almost innumerable living things, most of which are too small to be seen in a handful of dirt. Water is a simple compound, but we are not likely to encounter it as such. Many substances are dissolved in it, particles are suspended in it, and living creatures float and swim about in it. Everywhere we find mixtures of things, in a drop of pond water, a lump of soil, a breath of air, most things that man makes. Not only do we find mixtures of things everywhere; these things interact with one another because of processes of their own, changing one another and the conditions of the whole.

In this book of the series David Gates has dealt with one important facet of the interrelations between man and his environment. For each of these books, no matter what is the main focus (climate, energy, materials, waste, food, population, recreation, transportation, law, or aesthetics and the cultural roots of our viewpoints), we have asked the authors to take a holistic point of view and to write about interconnections, interactions, consequences, and, in fact, the systems of man and nature together. As broad-gauged thinkers and scientists, they are well equipped for this demanding goal.

Man has become the leading cause of environmental change. He is discovering that he is responsible for much that he does not like—air and water pollution, poisons in our food, deteriorated cities—and that in order to correct such disagreeable, unhealthy, and unpleasant conditions he must understand the ecology of his environmental interrelations.

Although this book can stand alone, it is also an integral part of the series on *Man and His Environment.*

John E. Bardach
Marston Bates
Stanley A. Cain

preface

Even today, in our highly technological modern world, man still is dependent upon climate and upon the weather. Most life on earth owes its existence to green plants, which depend for growth on the climate in which they are living. The entire food web and chain of life reacts in many subtle and intricate ways to the weather and climate of a region. The energy we use, the amount of coal and oil we burn, the insulation of our clothing and homes, the cost of snow removal, flood protection, and wind damage, the toll taken by hurricanes and tornadoes, the price we pay for global communication and worldwide transportation, all are inextricably dependent upon weather and climate.

The subject matter concerning man and climate is immense, and a treatise on this topic could continue indefinitely. I have chosen to limit the subject matter here to a few major categories and to select only particular examples within these categories. I have included many traditional topics, which are described in any book concerned with climate, but, at the same time, I have attempted to introduce some concepts, such as the idea of energy exchange between plants and animals and their environment, which are not often discussed in a book such as this. Climate is coupled to a plant or animal, including man, primarily through the flow of energy. Traditionally air pollution may not have been dealt with under the subject matter of climate, but it is now such a critical component of man's environment and so strongly linked to climate conditions that it fell quite naturally within the general topic of this book. In order to understand the climate of a region, one must understand the weather, and this requires visualization of the global circulation of the ocean, of air overhead, and of the differential solar heating of the earth from the equator to the poles.

Man inadvertently modifies climate by his own technological and agricultural activities. This is not new to modern man, but, as a result of his enormous expansion of industry, his population explosion, his massive use of the automobile, his worldwide air traffic, and his extension of agriculture to most regions of the earth, the effects of his activities upon climates are no longer strictly local but of global significance. Furthermore, the effects of man's activities on climate are no longer purely seasonal or of short duration, but some may persist for decades, hundreds of years, or longer. There appears to be a slow buildup in the concentration of carbon dioxide in the atmosphere. Carbon dioxide in the atmosphere comes into equilibrium with its concentration in the oceans only after several hundred years. For this reason the result of burning fossil fuels at a rapid rate tends to build up the amount of carbon dioxide in the air. Many fine particles or aerosols put into the air by man may be floating around the earth, year after year, and producing a change of climate by altering the earth's albedo, or reflectivity to solar radiation.

The citizen of the modern world must have a good understanding of his environment in order to maintain a viable habitat. He should appreciate the diversity of organisms, the beauties of natural history, the uniqueness of the earth's ecosystem, the fantastic synergisms which have evolved between life and atmosphere. From this appreciation should emerge a conscience within man to manage the earth's resources, to respect the limitations of air and water reservoirs, to limit his own population, and to realize that the diversity of organisms is indeed the life support system for man himself. It is my hope that the reader will realize these principles as a part of the experience gained from this book.

David M. Gates

man
and his
environment:
climate

introduction

Despite the fabulous advances in modern technology, man's well-being and sustenance is still utterly and completely at the mercy of climate. The more crowded the planet earth is with people and despite great technological advances, the more critical for survival is our dependence on the vagaries of climate. Crop production is still climate-controlled. A drought or flood can wipe out enormous areas of grain and fruit or affect the fodder and forage supplied to cattle. Poor storage of grains in underdeveloped countries results in enormous annual losses from climate, insects, and rats. Crop diseases and insect infestations are influenced strongly by climate. The presence of certain diseases affecting man's health, such as malaria, encephalitis, plague, cholera, schistosomiasis, and many others are influenced by climate. Mass transportation within large urban areas grinds to a halt when winter storms dump deep snows on the cities. Airplane traffic is grounded during periods of severe storms and thousands of people are affected by the consequences. Power and communication lines are knocked out by great storms, normal community activity is disrupted, and lives are often in jeopardy.

1

In fact, an old proverb from King Alfred goes something like this:

So it falls that all men are
With fine weather happier far.

An understanding of all the aspects of weather and climate is of great importance and can help us deal with the everyday as well as the dramatic effects of weather. Among the more dramatic and violent manifestations of weather are floods, blizzards, ice storms, hail, and other meteorological events. All of these can release incredibly large forces which can take an awesome toll of life and property. On 26 and 27 September 1954 a typhoon struck Japan and left 1700 people killed, 600 ships sunk, 100,000 Japanese homeless, and 20,000 buildings destroyed. In August 1970 a devastating hurricane hit Corpus Christi, Texas, causing the loss of several lives, injury to many, and a million dollars of damage. Only the use of a modern alert system prevented a much greater loss of life. A massive tropical storm struck the Ganges Delta region of East Pakistan on 13 November 1970, and the death toll exceeded 300,000. It is considered to have been one of the world's worst natural catastrophes.

What is it moulds the life of man?
    The weather
What makes some black and others tan?
    The weather
What makes the Zulu live in trees,
And Congo natives dress in leaves
While others go in furs and freeze?
    The weather

The successes and failures of man's migration and settlement are a record of the climates of the earth. Until recently settlement and population density remained low in those regions of the world where climates were too hot, too dry, or too cold. Only recently has man through air conditioning, irrigation, and commercial heating been able to increase substantially the population densities of these harsh regions. However, the often expressed concept that the Caucasian could not live and work effectively in the humid tropics may be quite wrong. Americans have settled the Panama Canal Zone, where they have remained for several generations, partly because they have vigorously modified the environment by building roads, draining swamps, eliminating insects, and building shaded, well-ventilated houses.

Climate may be defined as the characteristic weather conditions of a given place, a specific locale or region, averaged over an extended period of time. If average weather conditions make up climate, then obviously to understand climate we must also understand *weather*, which may be defined as the general atmospheric conditions (temperature, humidity, precipitation, winds, radiation, and any other meteorological events) at a given place at any time. Climate and weather are both made up of dynamic processes. Both are constantly changing, from season to season, from day to night, and from moment to moment.

In studying climate we are usually concerned with regional climates. A plant or animal, on the other hand, may respond primarily to its *microclimate*. This was defined by Rudolph Geiger, the famous German climatologist, as "the climate near the ground," though I prefer to think of the microclimate as the climate, no matter how small, in the immediate vicinity of an object or organism. The agricultural productivity of a region depends on the regional climate, although each and every plant or animal contributing to that productivity responds specifically to the microclimate of its immediate vicinity. Of course the microclimate of a particular plant or animal in a valley, on a hill top, or in a field has a definite relation to the climate of the entire region, but nevertheless microclimates may vary considerably from the general climate. For instance, the climate of the arid southwestern United States is described as hot and dry during summer months, but there are microclimates along the water courses of that region which are hot and humid. The microclimate of plants growing along the

4

*man
and his
environment:
climate*

south side of a house may be warm and dry in winter, while
the regional climate is cold and moist. The weather which
occurs over a forest, across a meadow, or in the region generally does, of course, determine the climate of a tree top, of the
forest canopy, of the ground surface beneath the forest, of the
meadow surface, or of any other particular habitat. There are
times when the distinction between the terms "weather" and
"climate" will be difficult to discern, since climate is a time
average of the weather in the strict sense of the word. However, the distinction fades when we are concerned with short
intervals of time where averages are not always meaningful.

The environment of man includes all things physical and
biological as well as the interaction of groups of people with
one another. Climate is one significant part of our environment, a part which pertains primarily to the flow of air about
us and the character of the earth's surface. Climate is described
in terms of certain parameters, air temperature, wind, humidity, rainfall, snow, ice, and radiation (sunlight, skylight, reflected light, and radiant heat). Climate interacts with an
organism through the flow of energy between the organism
and the environment. All life depends upon energy—metabolic
energy, muscular energy, energy to drive nerve impulses to the
brain, light for vision, warmth, and heat, energy by which to
grow, to multiply, to move about, and energy by which to
breathe, and energy may flow from one object to another by
radiation, conduction, convection, evaporation, and mechanical
transfer. Radiation is the flow of energy in the form of electromagnetic waves known as light, ultraviolet, or x-rays, infrared
heat, or radio waves.

Infrared heat is essential for warmth, and the visible wavelengths known as "light" are also essential to vision. Ultraviolet rays can act favorably to tan our skins and generate vitamin D, while at other times they cause severe sunburn and
illness. Wind forces the movement of air across our bodies. If
the air is cold we lose energy by convection, and if the air is hot
we gain energy by the same process. In the winter we speak of
"wind chill factors." This measures the relative cooling power
of the winter winds. We protect our bodies against undue heat

loss when subjected to large chill factors by wearing insulating clothing. Some animals cope with the winter cold by hibernating in warmer burrows underground, while other animals escape the heat of summer by burrowing beneath the soil surface.

The humidity of the air affects our comfort. We may perspire profusely in the dry air of the desert, and we may be wet, sticky, and uncomfortable in the humid air of the tropics. All animals lose water through respiration and perspiration, while plants lose water by *transpiration*, the emission of water as vapor through the pores of plant foliage. It is this loss of water that often keeps them cool and comfortable. In fact, the ability to lose water freely often spells the difference between death and survival for an organism in a hot environment. Some plants become dormant when conditions are extremely dry and they remain so until favorable rains cause them to grow, flower, and set seed. Desert flowers bloom profusely when stimulated by spring rains and moderate temperatures. The movement of water through plants carries a stream of essential nutrients to the food-producing chloroplasts within leaves and other tissues.

All life on earth is intimately and inescapably coupled to its surrounding climate. A wave of verdant green moves northward from the Gulf Coast across the continent of North America as spring brings moderate temperatures, longer days, more sunshine, and favorable rains. Flowers bloom, insects emerge from their winter sanctuaries in soils, streams, lakes, and woods. Birds migrate northward, and the landscape becomes colorful and more active once again. Not that winter is dull and static, for even in the far North life is active above as well as beneath the white snow cover across the land. Evergreens grow and continue photosynthesis during the winter; arctic owls, foxes, caribou, wolves, lemmings, and many other animals thrive during the dark, cold days and nights of the winter season. But as temperatures rise and rays of sunshine slant across the valleys, mountains, and plains, the pulse of life quickens and organisms continue their life cycles of birth, growth, and death. Each plant or animal shares with all the others the available energy, space, and time of these more favorable periods. In many regions of the world, such as the southern and central states of the United States, the time of optimum growth and activity is long, while in the North it is shorter, and in the deserts it is extremely brief or nonexistent for lack of water. Certain tropical and subtropical regions are favored by warmth and water throughout the entire annual cycle. This is reflected by abundant growth and a large diversity of plants and animals.

There is a law in ecology known as the law of tolerance which may be stated as follows: Any one or more of several factors when too scarce or too abundant may limit plant growth. The number of species become fewer as lands are drier, colder, or with shorter seasons of light and warmth. Tropical rain forests give way to the great deciduous forests of oak, hickory, ash, maple, beech, and other species across the eastern United States, which in turn relinquish their dominance to grasses across the more arid plains of the West, to sagebrush in the western intermountain basins, to cacti and succulents on the desert, and to coniferous forests in the northern United States and Canada. Mountains have their timberlines and *tundra* tops which are typified by treeless plains with low temperatures, a short growing season, and low precipitation. Tundra also dominates the landscape north of the Brooks Range in Alaska and of other very cold, windswept regions. Thus the character of the landscape is strongly climate-controlled throughout the world, and man is inexorably dependent upon the quality of this dynamic, living surface.

Climate means more to man than wind, water, heat, or cold, for it is also the quality of the ocean of air in which we live which has significance. Man depends upon sight to see and to find his way about the world. The visibility and clarity of the atmosphere is important to him both esthetically and physically. Man loses his way in a snowstorm or when fog blankets the ground. Haze cuts his visibility and restricts his activities. Man has a sense of smell, and the atmosphere has a characteristic odor to him. He recognizes the scent of ozone in the air near a thunderstorm, the fragrance of spring flowers, the attractive scent of oxides of nitrogen released by the respiration of soil bacteria, the "smell" of spring in the air, and the characteristic odors of the sea. Man is offended by the repugnant odors associated with the manufacture of his own exotic products, the plastics, metals, fuels, etc., of his industries. The plumes from our chimneys and the emissions of our automobiles are loading the global atmosphere with particulates and gases which are dirty, corrosive, smelly, and harmful to the health of all organisms, including ourselves. But worse than that there is increasing concern that worldwide climate is being affected by the pollution from our massive urban centers. We know for absolute fact that the climates within or near our cities are strongly affected by the pollutants in the air. If the global climate is indeed changed by our use of the atmosphere as a dilutant for our waste products, then mankind is confronted with a massive challenge to its survival. Whether the global climate becomes warmer or colder, beyond the normal, natural cycles and variations which have always characterized its trend, the consequences will be extremely difficult for mankind. One way or another crop production will be affected, sea levels will change, shorelines and estuaries will modify, stream flow and water tables will be affected, and man will have a desperate time attempting to manage the consequences. When the carrying capacity of the world ecosystem becomes loaded to its limit with humanity, then the system will become unusually sensitive to climate change and mankind will be vulnerable in a multitude of ways. It is critical that we understand these matters in order to deal with them in a rational, systematic manner while there is still time. This book is the story of climate as its affects man and as man affects it.

1
the
weather

The old adage, "Everybody talks about the weather, but nobody does anything about it," is no longer true. Scientists are working very hard on the problem of how to control the weather, how to modify it, and better yet how to understand it as thoroughly as possible. Hail suppression is accomplished through cloud seeding with silver iodide. This technique is successful in increasing precipitation under favorable circumstances. An urban area of concrete and asphalt, of buildings and parking lots, of freeways and streets greatly modifies the weather of its immediate surroundings. Just as we must understand the weather to understand climates, in order to control and modify the weather we must understand the processes which create it.

The winds of the world, or the movement of air masses, which differ in humidity and temperature, set up the climate patterns of the earth. The global winds are driven by solar radiation. Sunlight entering the earth's atmosphere is absorbed partially by the atmosphere and partially by land or ocean surface. Temperature and pressure differences between air masses give rise to air motion, and this motion is modified by friction with the earth's surface and by the rotation of the earth. If the earth were a smooth sphere, without oceans and land masses, and if it were heated uniformly, the circulation pattern of the earth's atmosphere would be almost entirely circumpolar along lines of latitude. But the differential absorption of sunlight between the land and ocean, the existence of massive ocean currents, such as the Gulf Stream and the Humboldt Current, and the rising of air masses over mountain barriers result in enormous disruptions of this simple circulation pattern. Equatorial air is heated more than polar air by sunlight, and this warmer air tends to move, in both hemispheres, toward the colder polar regions where it sinks.

If we look down on the North Pole of the earth from out in space, we see the great weather patterns of the Northern Hemisphere. The most striking feature about these patterns is their apparent wave motion about the pole. This circular or cyclonic motion is known as the *circumpolar vortex*. These massive cyclonic vortices exist in both the Northern and the Southern Hemispheres and dominate the flow pattern of westerly winds (winds that flow from the west) around the earth, from the poles to within 20° latitude of the equator.

When one begins to inspect the details of westerly winds and the circumpolar vortex, one finds an exceedingly complex picture of high- and low-pressure air masses which move in a complicated and often unpredictable manner. As the temperature changes, an air mass contracts or expands, and air pressure falls or rises. The regions of high pressure rush toward the regions of low pressure, creating wind. The general circulation of westerlies tends to be in latitudinal belts or zones, which also represent zones of climate. Because of certain geographic features, such as the shapes of continents and the positions of mountain ranges, the zonal character of wind flow and climate is modified, and climate abnormalities may occur. Most of the zonal weather features near the earth's surface have long been well known to sailors and navigators, and the circulation patterns of the stratosphere high above the ground are a part of common experience for jet pilots and aircraft navigators today.

pressure patterns

The pressure patterns of the atmosphere set up the winds of the world. In this way they affect the transport of moisture and in general are responsible for the weather we experience on the surface where we live. In order to understand weather and climate, we must know the pressure patterns of the earth.

Figures 1 and 2 show the average characteristic of sea-level pressure throughout the world for January and for July. It is immediately noticeable that the pressure pattern within the Southern Hemisphere is always less complicated than the pressure pattern within the Northern Hemisphere. This is because the Southern Hemisphere is dominated by oceans while the Northern Hemisphere has much more land mass in the form of continents. In January high-pressure systems, or air masses, dominate the continents, and low-pressure systems dominate the oceans. Generally in July the oceans are dominated by

figure 1. *Average sea-level pressure pattern for the world during January. The heavy alternately pecked and circled lines show zones of frequent frontal activity. (From Frederick K. Hare,* The Restless Atmosphere, *Hutchinson, London, 1966.)*

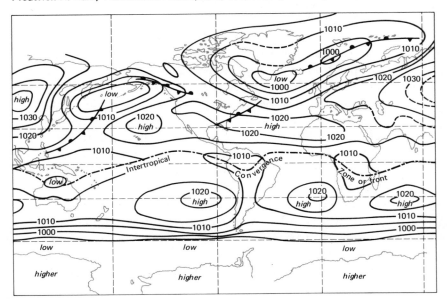

the weather

high-pressure systems and the continents by low-pressure systems. A low-pressure belt exists around the world at the equator, and in July it tends to shift north of the equator. This belt of low pressure is known as the belt of calms and to sailors as the *doldrums*. The primary circulation features of the earth's atmosphere are summarized below in the manner of F. K. Hare in his excellent book, *The Restless Atmosphere*.

southern hemisphere

1. In subtropical areas, about 30° latitude, a broad high-pressure belt exists throughout the year and is known as the subtropical high-pressure belt. In January this high-pressure belt tends to be mixed with small low-pressure systems over Australia and South Africa.

2. Throughout the temperate regions of the Southern Hemisphere the pressure falls steadily toward the south and reaches a minimum over Antarctica.

figure 2. *Average sea-level pressure pattern for the world during July. (From Frederick K. Hare,* The Restless Atmosphere, *Hutchinson, London, 1966.)*

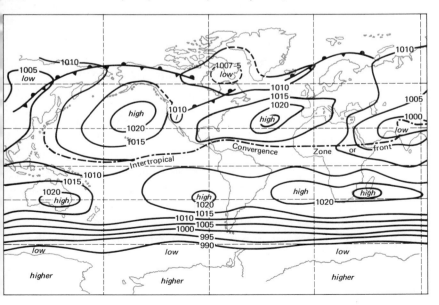

northern hemisphere

1. The subtropical high-pressure belt occurs over the oceans in January at latitudes around 30°N but connects up with more intense high-pressure systems in higher latitudes over the continents. The subtropical high-pressure belt of the Northern Hemisphere is primarily over the oceans, whereas in the Southern Hemisphere it encircles the globe. In July, high-pressure systems dominate the north Atlantic Ocean and the north Pacific Ocean at mid-latitudes.

2. The subarctic low-pressure system is well-developed in January and affects much of the weather of the Northern Hemisphere during the winter. It consists of two great low-pressure regions, one over Iceland and the other over the Aleutian Islands, separated by a relatively high-pressure system over the North Pole. In July the low-pressure systems are weaker, the Aleutian center has disappeared, and the Iceland center is small, while pressure remains high over the pole. Again the subarctic system in the Northern Hemisphere does not extend in a uniform belt around the world as it does in the Southern Hemisphere.

3. The pressure systems of mid-latitude regions in the Northern Hemisphere are very broken up compared with those in the Southern Hemisphere. In winter there are large high-pressure regions over North America and Asia, and in summer there is a large low-pressure system centered over southern Asia.

winds of the world

Now we see that the pressure systems, along with the heating by solar radiation and the rotation of the earth, determine the pattern of winds on earth; that, generally speaking, winds will occur when there is a flow of air from regions of high pressure toward regions of low pressure; and that winds near the ground are strongly influenced by the presence of surface features, such as mountains, and the friction forces between the wind and the surface. In fact, the wind speeds near the ground are much smaller than speeds aloft. North of the equator the wind blows in such a way that an observer with his back to the wind finds the low pressure on his left, while south of the equator the low pressure is on his right. The pressure differences between high- and low-pressure systems would by themselves cause winds to blow in a direction perpendicular to lines of constant pressure, known as *isobars*, but because of friction forces and the rotation of the earth the winds often flow nearby along lines of constant pressure. Thus in a weather map of the United States the winds are shown flowing clockwise and outward from the center of a high-pressure system and counterclockwise and inward toward the center of a low-pressure system. In the Southern Hemisphere the winds will move counterclockwise around a high-pressure region and clockwise around a low-pressure region. A simplified drawing of the wind flow around high- and low-pressure systems in the earth's Northern and Southern Hemispheres is shown in Fig. 3.

figure 3. *Wind flow around high- and low-pressure systems in the Northern and Southern Hemispheres.*

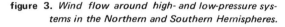

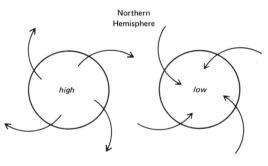

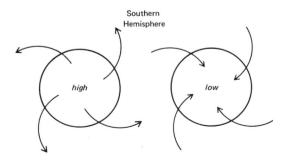

The winds of the world are highly significant, as they affect the climate of a region. Wind direction is always specified as the direction from which the winds come. Hence, westerlies are winds blowing from the west toward the east. A southerly wind blows from the south toward the north. The general wind belts are summarized as follows:

1. In the doldrums winds are light and ascending currents of air near the equator which produce convective cloudiness with precipitation. This is because warm, moist air rises, and as it mixes with cooler air aloft the moisture condenses out.

From the "Rime of the Ancient Mariner" by Samuel Taylor Coleridge we have a description of the doldrums:

Down dropt the breeze, the sails dropt down,
'Twas sad as sad could be;
And we did speak only to break
The silence of the sea!

All in a hot and copper sky,
The bloody Sun, at noon,
Right up above the mast did stand,
No bigger than the Moon.

Day after day, day after day,
We stuck, nor breath nor motion;
As idle as a painted ship
upon a painted ocean.

2. The trade winds prevail north and south of the equator to about 30° latitude. They blow from the northeast and are called the northeast trade winds in the Northern Hemisphere, and they blow from the southeast in the Southern Hemisphere. Warm air near the equator rises and circulates northward aloft, descending near the horse latitudes (30°) where it creates persistently clear skies. Descending or subsiding air undergoes an increase in pressure as it drops from high in the atmosphere toward the ground. This increase of pressure warms the air and results in unsaturated clear skies. The ascending air

near the equator cools and drops its moisture in the form of precipitation.

Here the Ancient Mariner did better as Coleridge writes:

The fair breeze blew, the white foam flew,
The furrow followed free;
We were the first, that ever burst
Upon that silent sea.

These were the trade winds which pushed the ship into the dead air of the doldrums, and this part of the verse precedes the description given above.

3. The prevailing westerlies on the poleward side of the subtropical high-pressure system are highly variable and tempestuous at latitudes of 30° to 60°. In the Northern Hemisphere the southwesterly winds of warm, moist air from the subtropics meet the northeasterly winds of cold, dry air from the Arctic between latitudes of 50° to 60°, along the meandering polar front to form a zone of cloudiness and precipitation. Stormy inconsistency and high variability characterize the climates of these parts of the world. Although generally temperate they are frequently invaded by sutropical or arctic climatic conditions.

4. From latitude 60° toward the poles in both the Northern and Southern Hemispheres of the earth there exist the polar easterlies, winds which blow from the east. The polar regions are dominated by relatively high-pressure systems.

temperature patterns

There are five general temperature zones on earth as follows: (1) Arctic—which is south from the North Pole to the place where the mean July temperature is 10°C (50°F); (2) North Temperate—from the southern boundary of the Arctic Zone to where the mean annual temperature is 20°C (68°F) or to the Tropic of Cancer; (3) Tropic or Torrid—which is south from the Tropic of Cancer to the place where the mean annual temperature in the Southern Hemisphere is 20°C (68°F) or to the Tropic of Capricorn; (4) South Temperate—from the Tropic of Capricorn to where the mean January temperature is 10°C (50°F); and (5) Antarctic—which is from the southern boundary of the South Temperate Zone south to the South Pole.

The Tropic or Torrid Zone is the hottest and has the least temperature variation. The 20°C (68°F) mean temperature line, or *isotherm*, coincides approximately with the limits of the trade winds in each hemisphere. The highest mean annual temperature of 30°C (86°F) exists in this zone in central Africa, India, the north of Australia, and in Central America. In general, the less the precipitation the higher the temperature. The highest air temperature recorded on earth, at the standard height above the ground, about 1.5 m (meters), was a temperature of 57.8°C (136°F) at Azizia in Tunisia. Higher air temperatures are found next to the soil surface, but when speaking of temperatures from a meteorological standpoint we must use the standard reference level. There are places in the western Sahara and in northwest India or Pakistan where the mean maximum temperature exceeds 45°C (113°F). Near the equator the maximum temperatures are not as high as they are at these other places. Seasonal changes in the tropics occur because of variations more often in precipitation than in temperature. There are dry deasons and wet seasons. The lowlands near the oceans are generally wetter, and the interior regions are drier with more variation of precipitation. Atmospheric pressure tends to be lowest near the equator. Pressure variations are small, winds are relatively low to calm, and heavy rains and thunderstorms are a general rule of the tropics. Most days are partly cloudy, except in desert regions, and the annual variation of the amount of sunlight is small.

The temperate regions of the world are the most intemperate with respect to climate variability. Across the temperate belts of the world, we find the greatest number of climate subdivisions. There are climates of the Mediterranean coastal type, which are warm, of modest temperature variation, and the most benign of all climates; the climates of continental interiors with dry, hot summers and cold winters; the mountain

*the
weather* climates, which vary from extremely dry and windy to relatively still and very wet. Temperature variations of temperate regions can be as much as 30°C (54°F) within a few hours, and variations of 15°C (27°F) are very common. Seasonal extremes range from winter lows of -40°C (-40°F) to summer highs of 45°C (113°F).

influence of continents

The pressure and wind patterns of the Northern Hemisphere are much more variable and irregular than they are in the Southern Hemisphere. This is because of the dominant presence of continents, in the Northern Hemisphere, where there are coast lines, mountain ranges, and vast interiors which strongly influence the pressure systems and wind patterns. Figure 4 shows the influence of the coast lines on the great circu-

Figure 4. *The prevailing ocean currents of the world from December to February. (From Handbook of* Meterology *by Frederic A. Berry* et al. *Copyright 1945 McGraw-Hill Book Company. Used with permission of McGraw-Hill Book Company.)*

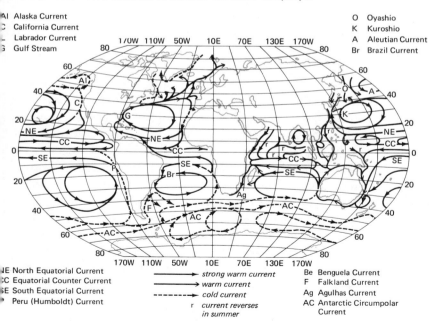

Al Alaska Current
C California Current
L Labrador Current
G Gulf Stream

O Oyashio
K Kuroshio
A Aleutian Current
Br Brazil Current

NE North Equatorial Current
CC Equatorial Counter Current
SE South Equatorial Current
P Peru (Humboldt) Current

⟶ *strong warm current*
⟶ *warm current*
------⟶ *cold current*
r *current reverses in summer*

Be Benguela Current
F Falkland Current
Ag Agulhas Current
AC Antarctic Circumpolar Current

lation patterns of the oceans—the Gulf Stream, the Japanese Current, the Humboldt Current, the Southern Equatorial Current, the Labrador Current, and many others. These currents, in turn, have great influence on the coastal climates of England, California, Peru, Australia, Labrador, and other regions. The interactions of air currents, caused by thermal contrasts between land and ocean, with the general circulation pattern are climatically very significant. In the daytime there is a thermal gradient from the warm land to the cooler sea; at night the gradient is reversed from the sea to the cooler land along the coast. At the surface this results in a sea breeze during the day and a land breeze at night, both of which have important effects upon coastal climate. The interiors of continents tend to become very hot in summer and very cold in winter. These great temperature extremes have significant influence on the pressure and wind systems in the heartlands of continents. In North America the Midwest is often dominated by a gigantic low-pressure system centered over the Mississippi Valley in which the climate is hot and stagnant without much air movement. This enormous low-pressure system is blocked to the East by the gigantic Bermuda high situated over the Atlantic Ocean.

influence of mountains

Mountain ranges affect the pressure patterns and wind systems in very special ways which are described in detail elsewhere. The windward sides of mountains are characterized by high precipitation, because here the air flow ascends and cools. The leeward sides of mountain ranges, those opposite the side from which the wind blows, are characteristically dry and relatively sunny, being in the so-called rain shadow of the mountains. The undulating flow of air over a mountain range has special features clearly associated with it, such as the lee-wave cloud and other flow patterns relatively close to the surface of the earth. The flow of air across a mountain barrier very much resembles the flow of water in a stream over rocks. There is a giant wave motion of the air on the leeward sides of mountains. The air movement is first deflected upward by the mountain range, then as it passes beyond the crest of the divide it sinks and falls rapidly but soon curves into a trough and is sent upward again. Thus it begins oscillating to form an extended wave pattern downwind from the mountains. This wave motion produces very strong alternate downdrafts and updrafts outward from the leeward slopes of the mountain barrier. Characteristic of this lee wave are long, lenticular clouds often seen in a clear sky parallel to the range of mountains or hills. Airplane pilots often used to encounter severe difficulties when flying toward the mountains on the leeward side, first encountering a strong updraft and then a severe downdraft. The result was disaster as the pilot would overcorrect his craft for the updraft and then be plunged into the mountain by the downward current of air. Today we understand this phenomenon and pilots are forewarned.

Those who have lived in mountain regions know well the *nozzle effect* of winds funneling through mountain canyons. Winds greater than 125 mph were recorded at Boulder, Colorado, in December 1968. Living at the mouth of a mountain canyon can be described as comparable to being at the end of a firehose. The air rushing across the Rocky Mountains becomes highly concentrated in some of the deep canyons and emerges from their lower ends at incredible speeds.

The great mountain barriers also influence the general circulation pattern considerably; for instance, the Alps and the Himalayas, running east and west, effectively block the flow of polar air toward the south. Hence northern Italy, southern Switzerland, and northern India are consistently warmer in winter than they would be if the mountains were not present.

The influence of continents on the flow of air is seen most dramatically in the Asiatic monsoons. During the winter months Siberia is a region of intense cold and high pressure, with the result that northerly and northeasterly winds flow across eastern Asia and stream out into the Bay of Bengal causing minimum cloudiness and precipitation over the land. During the summer the situation reverses, the interior is under the influence of a low-pressure system, and huge amounts of warm, moist tropical air flow off the Bay of Bengal and off the

Indian Ocean to cause enormous precipitation over parts of India and eastern Asia.

frontal systems

Fronts have been described as the "battle zones of the sky," and indeed they are. Fronts are where the action is. Fronts are the boundaries between warmer, lighter air masses and colder, heavier air masses. Just as cream rises to the top of milk because it is lighter, warm moist air rises above cold dry air. But not without protest, so to speak, and the result is turbulence and conflict causing storms of wind, clouds, and precipitation. The weather and climate of a region are direct consequences of frontal systems developing over that region.

There are several kinds of fronts. Anyone who watches weather reports on television is aware of the various kinds of fronts often described. What was at one time purely technical language, familiar only to the specialists, has now become language for the layman. There are cold fronts, warm fronts, and stationary fronts. If a mass of cold air is advancing toward a mass of warm air, the cold air will push itself in under the warm air and the zone of contact is recognized as a *cold front*. As the wedge of warm air is pushed up over the wedge of cold air, clouds form, usually altostratus and altocumulus, and precipitation may occur. If, on the other hand, a wedge of warm air advances over a wedge of cold air, and the air movement is primarily the movement of the warm air toward the cold air, we have what is known as a *warm front*. Usually the warm front develops over the trailing edge of a cold air mass. Since the trailing edge of cold air is often spread over quite a distance, the warm front is more dispersed than the cold front which forms along the abrupt leading edge of a cold air mass. Because of the abrupt change of temperature produced by the steep leading edge along a cold front, the storm activity there is usually much more violent than along the warm front. When either a warm front or a cold front shows little movement or wavers back and forth, it is called a *stationary front*.

Fronts are *always* associated with low-pressure systems or

depressions in the atmosphere. For this reason the winds blow counterclockwise in the Northern Hemisphere about the frontal surface. Our frontal systems enter the United States from northwestern Canada, where many of our winter storms originate. Some frontal systems develop within the United States east of the Rocky Mountains or in the Mississippi Valley, where moist gulf air mixes with polar air from the north. Frontal systems, once developed, usually move in a northeasterly direction, but sometimes they move in an erratic manner and in other directions as well. A cold front may extend up to 10,000 or 15,000 ft above the surface and have a forward range of movement of 15-20 mph. At this rate a major storm can dump snow or rain on much of a two-state area covering from 500 to 800 miles in a day. Usually the rate of movement of the storm front is not uniform.

Frontal systems which separate patterns of air flow across North America are of enormous significance. Zones of distinct vegetation types are separated by frontal systems. One mean annual frontal position occurs across northern California, northern Nevada, and into Utah, separating sage and grassland to the north from sage and saltbush desert to the south. During summer months there is a continuous flow of Pacific air which is subsiding and diverging as it flows eastward over northern California into Oregon and Washington. The sky above the high Sierras is phenomenally clear during periods when divergent Pacific air is flowing eastward. Suddenly as global patterns shift in the autumn, typhoon conditions occur over the Pacific and the whole pattern of eastward flow over the northwest coast changes from divergence to convergence and from falling, subsiding air to a condition of rising air. The famous 12 October Columbus Day storm slams into the northwest coast—some houses may lose roofs or shingles, flooding occurs, trees blow down, and often considerable damage results.

Over the Midwest other events occur which associate with the frontal lines of demarcation between warm, moist gulf air and cooler, drier northern air. Abruptly on or about 27 March the thunderstorm activity in the Midwest increases, as the frontal system which strikes a line approximately northeastward across the central United States, from near Fort Collins, Colorado, to the Saint Lawrence River in Canada, buckles northward. This occurs in the upper Midwest when the circumpolar vortex splits from three to four vortices. This movement brings moist air northward from the Gulf of Mexico and is responsible for the precipitation in Illinois, Missouri, and Iowa which makes the agricultural production of the corn belt possible. Further to the west conditions are drier, and corn gives way to wheat and the grassland prairies. The eastward extension of the original prairie, a slender wedge projecting into northern Illinois, was the result of an extension of this dry continental air flow during the driest years only. The prairie regions of Kansas, Nebraska, the Dakotas, and Manitoba are characterized by low snowfall in the winter, causing low moisture and little or no protective cover against the cold winter winds. The enormous Bermuda high-pressure system over the Atlantic Ocean blocks the eastward flow of moist gulf air and enhances the flow northward into the upper Midwest. The Pacific Ocean high-pressure system suddenly moves northward by about 5° latitude around 25 June and creates the subsiding air flow over the Sierra Nevada which was described in the last paragraph. It slowly moves southward again about 15 September, and around 5 November the Aleutian low forms again to the North. It is in the Aleutians that many of our winter storms are bred.

These winter storms strike tracks across the upper midwest and dump snow from Oregon and Washington across Wyoming, the Dakotas, into Michigan, and eastward. Polar air dominates the situation north of the winter polar front, which dips in a great arc, more or less parallel to the Canadian border and into the lower Great Lakes. This southern boundary of winter polar air generally coincides with the southern boundary of spruce and fir forest. During the summer months the polar front moves northward into Canada, and the northern boundary of the spruce and fir forest appears to coincide with its position.

weather and climate

Thus it is weather that makes the climates of the world. The weather is fueled by radiation from the sun, which warms the earth's atmosphere and ground surface. The earth then reradiates heat to space. If this were not so, the earth would simply become warmer and warmer. Radiational cooling and solar heating create temperature differentials between ocean and land, and between the equator and the poles. Temperature differentials in the atmosphere create pressure systems which generate winds and air movement. Moisture is evaporated by sunshine from the ocean and land surfaces only to rise into the sky, condense, and rain on the land and oceans once again. Radiation, air temperature, wind, and moisture make up the parameters of weather and thus create the conditions of climates throughout the world.

2
climate
factors

Our goal in this book is not only to understand the physical phenomena of climate but to realize how climate affects man, plants, and animals. We also wish to know how the activities of man influence climates and how these, in turn, react upon the plant and animal communities of the world. Man's well-being and survival in the future may depend critically upon his success in understanding these subtle and complex relationships. When we attempt to understand the influence of climate on an organism, we are forced to ask ourselves the following questions: What are the significant climate factors? What do they have in common? How do they influence the organism? We have described the various types of weather situations and the fact that they give rise to certain types of climates. We will see how we can classify climates so that we have some idea of their significance with respect to plant growth, the types of plant communities which may occur naturally, or even with respect to the comfort of man. But how precisely is each organism, whether plant or animal, coupled to its climate and microclimate? It is by the transfer of energy between the organism and its environment.

All organisms require energy to live. All organisms, in order to survive, must stay within certain temperature limits, and energy is required to maintain specific temperature conditions. Energy is defined as the ability to do work, and work is done whenever a force acts on some object, displacing it a certain distance. Therefore work is done when cells grow and expand, when new proteins are built, when electrons move in photosynthesis, when translocation, the conduction of soluble material within a plant, occurs, when blood is pumped through veins or arteries, or when any event of life takes place. Whenever work is done, energy is consumed. Energy must flow to an organism from the environment and from food. For green plants the availability of energy is determined by the amount of sunlight and moisture, and therefore by the climate.

The climatic factors of significance in this energy flow are radiation (including sunlight), air or water temperature, wind, and humidity. Other factors which might influence energy exchange, but which are generally insignificant, are electric, magnetic, and gravitational fields. Energy is exchanged between an organism and its environment by processes of radiation, convection, conduction, and evaporation of moisture. In order to understand how climate and organisms interact it is necessary to understand these processes of energy flow. Figure 5 illustrates the radiative energy flow between an organism and its environment.

radiation

Sunlight and skylight are a part of our everyday experience. We realize that the pulse of life on our planet is regulated by the diurnal sweep of the sun's rays across the surface of the rotating earth. We know that climate is closely coupled to the amount of sunlight present in any place at a given time, and that the color of the sky usually reveals the weather conditions at that moment and forecasts the weather to follow. Weather lore is filled with words of weather wisdom. From Shakespeare we have:

Men judge by the complexion of the sky,
The state and inclination of the day.

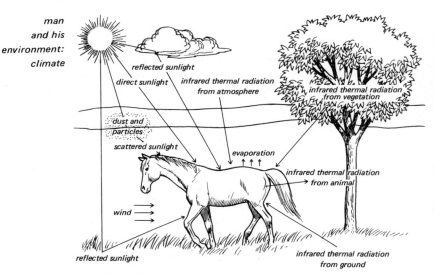

reflected sunlight

direct sunlight   infrared thermal radiation
from atmosphere

infrared thermal radiation
from vegetation

dust and
particles

scattered sunlight

evaporation

infrared thermal radiation
from animal

wind

reflected sunlight

infrared thermal radiation
from ground

figure 5. *Streams of radiative energy flowing between an animal and the environment. (From* Topics in the Study of Life: The Bio Source Book, *Harper & Row, New York, 1971, p. 388.)*

And of course we all remember:

*Sky red in the morning
Is a sailor's true warning;
Sky red at night
Is the sailor's delight.*

   Radiation has already been defined as energy which is propagated as an electromagnetic wave through space or through a medium such as air or water. Most media transmit only certain wavelengths of radiation and absorb others. Air absorbs ultraviolet and certain infrared wavelengths but transmits well the visible wavelengths of the spectrum, a good deal of the infrared, and a little of the ultraviolet. Water transmits none of the infrared, only some of the visible, and very little of the ultraviolet. A red piece of glass transmits only red wavelengths and absorbs all other visible wavelengths, as well as the ultraviolet and the infrared wavelengths. We know radiation of various kinds as everyday experience. We feel some radiation as heat and see some radiation as visible light. Radiation travels in a vacuum at the speed of light (3×10^{10} cm sec^{-1} (centimeters per second)).

streams of radiation

Outdoors there are many streams of radiation. These are illustrated in Fig. 5. Radiant heat is emitted by the ground surface and by objects, such as trees or the walls of buildings. Direct sunlight if the sun is high in the sky, as at noon in the summer, may be quite intense (1.2 to 1.4 cal cm^{-2} min^{-1} (calories per square centimeter per minute) is not uncommon). If the sun is low in the sky, or if the sky is hazy, the light emitted may be very weak (say about 0.4 cal cm^{-2} min^{-1}). Part of the sunlight entering the earth's atmosphere is scattered by the molecules and dust of the sky. This is the blue skylight which we see on clear days. The skylight may contribute about 0.2 cal cm^{-2} min^{-1} to the energy flux at the ground. Sunlight is reflected off the ground surface and from various objects. The intensity of the reflected sunlight depends on the nature of the reflecting surface. Typical amounts are from 0.1 to 0.3 cal cm^{-2} min^{-1}. The clear atmosphere itself will emit infrared radiant heat, but in relatively small amounts. It is the carbon dioxide and water vapor molecules in the clear atmosphere which radiate. Typical amounts from the clear sky are between 0.3 and 0.5 cal cm^{-2} min^{-1}.

sunlight and skylight

The planet earth is in orbit around a very hot star which we call the sun. The sun radiates a broad spectrum of ultraviolet radiation, light, and heat. The amount of sunlight reaching the earth varies during the year because of the slightly elliptical orbit of the earth around the sun. However, on the average, the amount of direct solar radiation received on a surface outside of the earth's atmosphere, perpendicular to the sun's rays, and at the mean distance of the earth from the sun, is 1.94 cal cm^{-2} min^{-1}. This quantity is known as the *solar constant*. It is one of the most important of all fundamental quantities known to man. All life on earth depends on the solar constant remaining more or less steady with time. We know that the quantity of ultraviolet radiation emitted by the sun varies with solar activity, but fortunately the total amount of energy radiated by the sun appears to change very little with time.

However, the amount of sunlight which reaches an object on the earth's surface varies enormously according to the transparency of the atmosphere, the amount of cloud cover, the position of the object on the earth, and the time of year. It is interesting to note the variation of direct sunlight which is incident upon a horizontal surface as a function of the time of year. Since atmospheric conditions are tremendously variable, and since we wish first to realize the influence of the position of an observer on earth relative to the sun, we see in Fig. 6 the amount of direct sunlight incident on a horizontal surface located outside of the earth's atmosphere. At the equator the seasonal variation of incident sunlight is slight, while at 80° north latitude, only 10° from the North Pole, the amount of sunlight incident upon a horizontal surface is zero in the win-

figure 6. *Amount of direct sunlight incident on a horizontal surface at the outer extremity of the earth's atmosphere as a function of the time of year for latitudes of 0°, 40°, and 80°.*

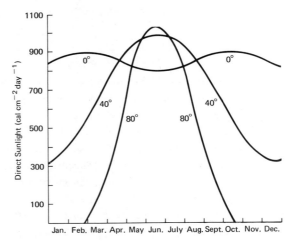

ter and very high during midsummer. At $40°$ north latitude, near where many of us live in the coterminous states, the variation of solar irradiation is great from winter to summer, but at the same time there is always a considerable quantity of potential sunlight. Only dense cloud cover will reduce the relatively low winter values to substantially smaller quantities at the surface. It is interesting to note that the midsummer values of solar irradiation of a horizontal surface are greater at high latitudes than at middle or low latitudes. The relatively constant temperatures of the tropics from summer to winter are a direct consequence of the nearly steady radiation regime throughout the year. Above the Arctic Circle or the Antarctic Circle there is continuous sunlight during midsummer. The result is that in these regions there can be very warm conditions with much radiation during midsummer, but six months later it can be intensely cold without any warmth whatsoever from the direct sunlight. The climates of the earth are very closely coupled to the radiation regimes of various parts of the planet. This can be best appreciated by understanding Fig. 6.

The primitive, primordial atmosphere which enveloped the earth before life began more than 3 billion years ago contained no oxygen and was highly transparent to ultraviolet radiation from the sun. As the simplest plants in the ocean began to photosynthesize, they released oxygen into the air and the oxygen molecules were broken by the action of sunlight to form ozone. The ozone diffused into the stratosphere high above the surface of the earth where it acted as a filter which absorbed ultraviolet radiation and shielded the surface from the intense ionizing rays of the sun. This afforded protection to life on the surface and the plants emerged from the ocean to spread a green photosynthesizing surface on the land. As photosynthesis increased in amount, more oxygen was released by the plants, more ozone was formed by photochemical action, and more protection against ultraviolet radiation was afforded to the surface. Animals evolved, breathing in oxygen and releasing carbon dioxide through respiration. The carbon dioxide present in the primitive atmosphere was an essential ingredient to photosynthesis. However, carbon dioxide and water vapor in the skies of the world began to play another important role. They formed a protective screen against the loss of too much radiant heat from the earth's surface to the cosmic cold of space. Carbon dioxide and water vapor each possess strong absorption bands at infrared wavelengths, precisely at those wavelengths in the spectrum in which the earth radiates its surface warmth outward toward space. The radiant heat from the surface is absorbed by the carbon dioxide and water vapor molecules in the atmosphere. They in turn radiate roughly half of the energy they absorb into space, and half is returned toward the earth.

So for nearly three billion years there has been a close, intimate cooperation between the evolution of life on the earth's surface and the development of the earth's atmosphere as we know it today. The oxygen released from plants by photosynthesis is not only the life support system for the metabolism of most animals, but, by forming ozone, it creates a screen against ultraviolet radiation on the short wavelength side of the spectrum. At the same time the protective blanket of carbon dioxide, so essential for the process of photosynthesis, retains the warmth of the ground on earth and allows the proper temperature to exist by absorbing the infrared rays. There is a small, clear window to space between the region of ultraviolet and infrared opacity through which sunlight streams to the surface and out through which we see to the planets and stars beyond. This is a unique, preciously balanced system between life, land, and sky upon which our existence inexorably depends.

The broad spectrum of sunlight passing through the earth's atmosphere to its surface is scattered by the molecules and dust of the sky and absorbed selectively, the ultraviolet by oxygen, ozone, and nitrogen, the infrared by carbon dioxide and water vapor. The spectral distribution of sunlight and skylight after it has penetrated the atmosphere is shown in Fig. 7. All ultraviolet shorter than $0.29\,\mu$ (microns) is removed by the atmosphere, and the infrared wavelengths are strongly attenuated. It is evident that skylight is relatively rich in ultraviolet and in blue wavelengths, but it is relatively depleted of red

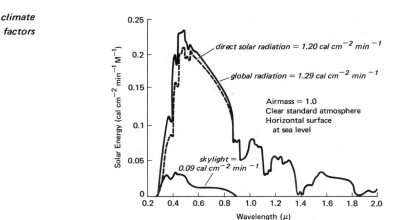

figure 7. *The spectral distribution of global radiation as a function of the wavelength. The global radiation is the sum of direct sunlight and scattered skylight.*

and near infrared, while most of the infrared spectrum is absent from skylight. We should remind ourselves that the visible spectrum, which is the wavelength span of light to which the human eye is sensitive, extends from 0.40 to 0.70 μ. Within the visible spectrum, we see colors as violet, indigo blue, green, yellow, orange, and red, in that order from the short to the long wavelengths. The ultraviolet is that part of the spectrum shorter than 0.40 μ and the infrared is comprised of those wavelengths greater than 0.70 μ. The human eye sees the skylight as blue and the direct sunlight as white to yellowish in color. When the sun is low on the horizon, more of the short wavelengths are scattered from the direct solar beam into the skylight, and the sun appears to be red or deep red, as it does at sunset or sunrise. When clouds cover the sky, all the infrared components of the sun's rays are absorbed by the water droplets in the clouds, and the ultraviolet and visible wavelengths are scattered strongly and diffusely to give a generally whitish or grayish appearance to the overcast sky. Dust and aerosols in the sky scatter and diffuse the incident sunlight, reflect more of it to space, and change the spectral composition of the sunlight which reaches the earth's surface. The spectral quality of sunlight and skylight has enormous influence on the behavior of life. Photosynthesis of plants and the response of plants and animals to light depends upon the total amount of solar radiation, the length of the day, and the spectral composition of the radiative fluxes at the ground.

blackbody radiation

All surfaces emit energy in the form of radiation in proportion to the fourth power of their absolute surface temperature. This physical law was discovered nearly one hundred years ago, first empirically by Josef Stefan, and then it was derived from theory by Ludwig Boltzmann. This law is known as the blackbody radiation law and is so ubiquitous and so fundamental that we will write it explicity here. The amount of radiation R, expressed in calories per square centimeter per minute, is proportional to the fourth power of the surface temperature T_s, measured in degrees Kelvin.

$$R = \sigma T_s^4 \qquad (1)$$

where $\sigma = 8.13 \times 10^{-11}$ cal cm^{-2} °K^{-4} min^{-1} is a proportionality constant.

A *blackbody* is defined as an object which has a perfectly "black" absorbing surface which absorbs all incident light or radiation and is therefore a perfect radiating surface. Surfaces are not perfectly black; in fact, very few even approach "blackness." Most surfaces absorb only some fraction of the incident radiation. The radiation absorbed must be reradiated if there is no other process for getting rid of the energy. According to another law of physics, first stated by Kirchhoff, a good absorber must be a good emitter at the same wavelength. What is in fact stated is that an object which absorbs a certain fraction of incident energy of a given wavelength must emit a similar fraction at the same wavelength. An object may absorb some fraction of the incident light of visible wavelengths and reradiate it as heat in the infrared. An object can have an absorptivity to visible wavelengths of say 40% and have an emissivity to infrared wavelengths of 98%. This does not contradict Kirchhoff's law, stated above, that a good absorber must be a good emitter at the same wavelength. You can stand in the sunlight and be warmed by the incident radiation absorbed by your clothing and skin. Although a portion of the incident sunlight which you absorb is visible light, you will reradiate this energy entirely as infrared radiant heat. Each one of us radiates approximately 70 W (watts) when resting and 260 W when active, depending on the surface temperature of our clothing and exposed skin. However, we must radiate more energy when we are standing in the sun than we do when we are in the shade since our surface temperature is somewhat warmer in the sun than in the shade.

thermal radiation

All surfaces emit radiant energy by virtue of their surface temperature. Although most surfaces do not radiate with the efficiency of a blackbody, they do emit a definite fraction of the radiant heat which a blackbody at the same temperature would radiate. Not only do our bodies radiate heat but so do all objects, such as the walls of a room, table surfaces, chairs, the ground, and clouds. The many streams of radiation striking an organism have been illustrated in Fig. 5. Thermal radiation, which refers to the radiation from all of the surfaces of organisms, rock, soil, walls, or clouds at their ambient temperatures, is truly ubiquitous in the world in which we live. In contrast to sunlight, which has much visible light and some ultraviolet and infrared, the thermal radiation consists of long-wave infrared wavelengths and only in the part of the spectrum from 4 to 10 to 30 μ and beyond. If you stand near a radiator or near a potbellied stove, you receive radiant energy which you cannot see as visible light but which you can feel as heat.

If you have watched a campfire die down and cool off, you are aware of the fact that there is a distinct change in the color of the flame or the color of the coals as it cools. When the fire is blazing vigorously, the flame is yellowish, or even whitish, in appearance, and much light and heat are given off. As the fire dies down the flame and coals become more red and give off less light and slightly less heat. After a while the flame disappears, the coals become dull red in appearance, then a darker red, and finally they glow no more. Light is no longer emitted from the warm coals, but heat continues to be given off. The warmth of the coals is felt for hours as radiated heat or infrared radiation, but it is not seen as light. We learn in the chemistry laboratory that the white flame from the Bunsen burner is very hot, and that a yellow flame is less hot. The physicists discovered that all objects emit radiation, and that this radiation varies with the temperature of the object. This temperature dependence can be observed in the wavelength of the emitted radiation: The higher the temperature of the object, the shorter the wavelength emitted. An object at room temperature, such as a wall, a desk, or a chair, will emit a broad spectrum of infrared wavelengths with a maximum intensity at a wavelength of approximately 10 μ. Room temperature would be at about 300°K (27°C) or a little less. If the temperature were doubled, say to 600°K (327°C), the object would still emit infrared wavelengths only, but the peak intensity would shift to 5 μ. If the absolute temperature were doubled again to 1200°K (927°C), the peak radiation would occur at 2.5 μ with a broad distribution out into the very long-wave infrared and also to shorter wavelengths, including the visible (0.4-0.7 μ). A source at this temperature would be visible to the human eye as a dull red glow. At a temperature of 2400°K (2127°C) the peak intensity is at a wavelength of 1.25 μ, and the object is seen in the visible spectrum as white hot, incandescent.

The climate of the world is largely moderated by the streams of radiation from various surfaces. In a room in your home there are infrared radiant fluxes from the walls, the floors and ceilings, and objects in the room. We receive from the walls at 68°F (20°C) about 0.6 cal cm^{-2} min^{-1} of radiant energy. This is a very significant quantity of heat reaching our body and has a great deal to do with our comfort in our homes. If the walls of a building are very cold but the air is warm, the room will be very uncomfortable because of a lack of sufficient radiation. Walls at 50°F (10°C) will emit only 0.52 cal cm^{-2} min^{-1}, and although this is only 0.08 cal cm^{-2} min^{-1} less than at 68°F, it nevertheless is sufficiently less to make one feel very cold and uncomfortable. For many people even 68°F is not enough, and they would rather have their rooms at about 75°F (24°C), from which they would derive about 0.63 cal cm^{-2} min^{-1} of energy.

irradiation of slopes

Since the radiation environment is so important as a part of our climate and the climate of plants and animals, it is necessary to consider how much sunlight various surfaces will receive as a function of the time of day. As a basis for comparison it might be pointed out that the solar constant is 1.94 cal cm^{-2} min^{-1}. There are special conditions at the earth's surface so that a horizontal surface may be irradiated by an amount of energy greater than the solar constant. In the Alpine tundra of the Rocky Mountains I have measured as much as 2.2 cal cm^{-2} min^{-1}, when the sky was very transparent and there were a few fleecy white cumulus clouds near the sun to reflect additional radiation to the surface. Usually a horizontal surface will receive from the sun direct irradiation, which is considerably attenuated by the atmosphere. Direct irradiation greater than 1.4 cal cm^{-2} min^{-1} is uncommon on clear days, and values as high as 1.6 cal cm^{-2} min^{-1} are experienced only at noon on the clearest days at high mountain locations. A north-facing wall has a completely different amount of incident sunlight than do south-facing, east-facing, or west-facing walls. Hillsides of differing slopes have various amounts of incident sunlight. The geometry of the sun, relative to any position on earth, is easily determined as a function of the time of day and the time of year. Figure 8 shows the amount of direct sunlight which is received on various slopes as a function of the time of day at 40° north latitude for three dates during the year, 22 December, 21 March, and 22 June—the winter solstice, spring equinox, and summer solstice. The situation at the time of the autumn equinox, 21 September, is the same as shown for the spring, or vernal, equinox.

Let us consider the character of the curves shown in Fig. 8 beginning with the summer solstice on 22 June. For a hori-

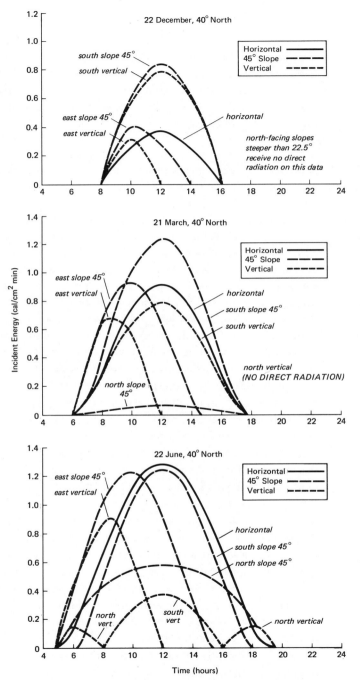

figure 8. *The amount of direct solar radiation incident upon sloping surfaces as a function of t time of day at latitude 40° N for the winter and summer solstice and the vernal equinc*

zontal surface, sunrise occurs at about 0500, but the amount of incident sunlight on the ground is very little at first because of the tangential angle of the sun's rays. By midday the horizontal surface is receiving the maximum amount of incident solar radiation, i.e., about 1.3 cal cm^{-2} min^{-1}. An east-facing $45°$ slope and an east-facing vertical slope receive the most immediate increase in illumination following sunrise. The quantity of sunlight incident upon them increases quickly during the early morning hours. However, "solar noon," or maximum intensity, is realized for the vertical and $45°$ slopes at 0830 and 1000, respectively. "Sunset" for these slopes is at 1200 and 1500, respectively. The horizontal surface has illumination throughout the day, although the bell-shaped curve causes the irradiation to be less in the early morning and late day than it is for some of the more vertical east-facing slopes. A vertical north-facing slope is illuminated by the rising sun on the summer morning, but its "day" of direct illumination is short, and the peak illumination occurs at 0600 and "sunset" by 0800. Although the vertical north-facing wall goes into the shadow of the sun at 0800, the vertical south-facing slope has its "sunrise" at this time. As one would expect, the vertical south-facing wall has maximum illumination at 1200. What happens during the afternoon is symmetrical with the morning, except that the events which took place for the east-facing wall during the morning are now true for the west-facing wall during the afternoon.

On 21 March and 21 September the vertical north-facing wall has no direct illumination by the sun, and the horizontal surface and south-facing slopes always have maximum illumination at midday, as they do at all times of the year. But now, instead of the horizontal surface having the greatest midday irradiance of all slopes, the $45°$-south-facing slope has the maximum, the horizontal the intermediate, and the vertical south-facing the least. By midwinter, at the time of the winter solstice, sunrise is at 0800 at $40°$ north latitude and all north-facing slopes steeper than $22.5°$ have no direct sunlight incident upon them at any time of the day. In midwinter the horizontal slope has less irradiation than either the south-facing vertical or the 45° slope to the south.

Many examples of the influence of slope and exposure can be found in nature and in association with man's activities. If one drives west from Denver, Colorado, into the mountain valleys, it is evident that the vegetation of the south-facing slope on the right is strikingly different from that of the north-facing slope on the left. The south-facing slope, which is more sunlit, drier, and warmer, is sparsely covered with juniper, ponderosa pine, and grasses. The north-facing slope, which is less sunlit, wetter, and cooler, is densely covered with spruce, fir, and grasses. The two completely different vegetation types meet in the bottom of the canyon where they are separated by maples, willows, and poplars growing along the edges of the mountain stream. Hillsides everywhere show similar differences in their vegetation cover. Douglas fir in the mountains of Wyoming will grow at much lower altitudes on north-facing slopes than on south-facing slopes, while mountain mahogany growing in the lower woodland communities will extend its range far up the mountain on south exposures. Often in the mountains of Europe and in other parts of the world one will notice north-facing slopes or, more accurately, poleward-facing slopes, to be covered with conifers and the opposite slopes with deciduous trees. Snow will accumulate and lay longer on north-facing slopes than on south-facing slopes. Soil temperatures near the surface will be 10°C (18°F) different between north- and south-facing slopes. A change in slope toward the north by 5° will reduce soil temperatures as much as a change of 300 miles latitude to the north would.

In Wisconsin, for example, the length of the growing season is 153 days on southwest-facing slopes compared with 147 days on northeast-facing slopes. In addition, the effect of a southwest slope could offset an increase of elevation as much as 700 ft. In Indiana the mesophytic beech–maple–tulip-poplar generally occupies north-facing slopes, and the oaks and hickories occupy south-facing slopes. In the northwest part of the United States relatively little germination of Douglas fir

seed occurs on south or southwest slopes, and no live seed-
lings which do get started survive after the first of August.
White oak in Ohio is found to prefer northeast exposures. Ivy
will grow well on a north-facing vertical wall, and not at all on
the opposite side. Grasses and vines growing on the slopes of
sand dunes along shorelines will grow abundantly on northern
exposures, and poorly or not at all on southern exposures.
Vineyards do best on hillsides with southern exposures. In addition, many vineyards will have stone walls which run hori-
zontally across the steep mountain sides, and the grapes grow
in rows at the base of each wall. These walls reflect additional
sunlight and warmth to the grapes, which enhances their development and improves the quality of the wine. It is also a
fact that vineyards growing above the shores of lakes benefit
from the extra light reflected from the water. Very often the
character of a hillside is seen in the community of mosses and
lichens, which grow on the surface. The keen observer needs
only look about him, when he is in the country, and note the
striking differences which occur on various slopes.

air temperature

The temperature of the air is a measure of its heat content.
As in the case of evaporation of moisture, *convection* and *conduction* are processes of heat transfer. Sensible heat flows
through a substance from higher to lower temperatures. Conduction is the direct transfer of heat from one substance to another. In our discussion here we are concerned with the conduction of heat from water, land, or an object to the air.
Convection is the transfer of heat by the circulation of fluid
(liquid or gas). This circulation is generated by differences in
temperature and density. The air near a source of heat becomes warm and therefore less dense. It is then compelled to
rise by the cold air nearby, which replaces it and is then
warmed in its turn. If the air is warmer than an organism or
object, heat will flow from the air to the organism by convection and conduction; if the air is cooler than an organism, heat
will flow from the organism by convection and conduction.

Therefore, the significance of air temperature to ourselves and to other living things is seen in the context of energy flow, in this case heat transfer.

Temperature may be measured with a mercury or alcohol thermometer, with a thermocouple, bolometer, or with other thermometric devices. The temperature scale with which we are most familiar in America is the Fahrenheit scale, established early in the eighteenth century by a German manufacturer of meteorological instruments, Gabriel Fahrenheit. He arbitrarily chose the melting point of ice to be $32°$ and the boiling point of water to be $212°$. A much more rational scale is the centigrade scale, whereby $0°$ is placed at the melting point of ice and $100°$ at the boiling point of water. Originally this scale was invented by the Swedish astronomer Andreas Celsius, also early in the eighteenth century. Celsius had elected to put the $100°$ point for melting ice and the $0°$ point for boiling water but his colleague, Marten Stromer, saw the wisdom of reversing the scale to the way it is now. The centigrade scale has fewer units than the Fahrenheit scale, each unit covering a wider temperature span. In this respect the Fahrenheit scale is more convenient because it is a somewhat finer measure of temperature. But a decimal system is usually preferred in general, and the centigrade scale is used worldwide for scientific work. In this book we shall give temperatures in both Fahrenheit and centigrade with a preference for the centigrade. The conversion from one to the other is given by the following formulas:

$$\frac{F° - 32}{180} = \frac{C°}{100} \tag{2}$$

$$F° = \frac{9}{5} C° + 32 \tag{3}$$

It is interesting to note that a temperature of $-40°C$ is equal to a temperature of $-40°F$ as well. A few other check points are convenient to keep in mind: $10°C = 50°F$, $20°C = 68°F$, $30°C = 86°F$, $40°C = 104°F$, and $50°C = 122°F$.

Late in the nineteenth century, physicists realized that there was such a thing as absolute zero, which is considered to be that temperature at which all molecular motion ceases. Experiments were made to show that the point of absolute zero was $273°C$ below the melting point of ice. On this basis the English physicist Lord Kelvin defined an absolute scale of temperature beginning with $0°K$ absolute zero. Hence:

$$K° = C° + 273 \qquad (4)$$

Actually, absolute zero is not exactly $273°$ below $0°C$ but is about $273.2°C$ below; however, for our purposes we can drop the fractional difference and use as a good approximation $-273°C$. It is only when we are considering the blackbody radiation laws that we must use the Kelvin scale. For all other purposes we can use the centigrade or Fahrenheit scales.

The air temperature varies enormously with locations on earth and with the seasons of the year. The air temperature usually referred to is measured inside a meteorological shelter or screen at a standard height of 1.5 m above the ground. The coldest standard air temperature ever recorded was $-88.3°C$ $(-127°F)$, measured at the Pole of Cold at the Soviet Vostok Station in Antarctica on 24 August 1960. The warmest standard air temperature ever recorded was $57.8°C$ $(136°F)$, measured at two places on earth, i.e., Azizia, Tunisia, on 13 September 1922 and San Luis, Mexico, on 11 August 1933. Higher air temperatures can be measured next to the soil surface, which in the case of a dark soil in full sun on a hot day can exceed $70°C$ $(176°F)$. Colder air temperatures are measured in the upper atmosphere, in the stratosphere, where temperatures as low as $-97°C$ $(-143°F)$ are recorded by instruments carried aloft by balloons. At altitudes of 50–60 miles above the ground, rocket-borne instruments have measured air temperatures lower than $-100°C$ $(-148°F)$, while at greater altitudes the temperature becomes progressively hotter until the "equivalent" temperature of the ionosphere is thousands of degrees centrigrade.

wind

"Every wind has its weather." (Bacon)

We refer to the motion of the air as wind. The movement of air over our surface, or over the surface of any organism, enhances the convective exchange of heat. A cold wind removes heat from our bodies, and a warm wind delivers heat to our bodies. To a considerable extent the agreeableness of a climate depends upon the amount of wind present, in addition to the amount of radiation. In order to understand climates, we must understand the origin and nature of wind.

High in the atmosphere, where the air is thin and man travels only by jet aircraft, there are strong westerly winds, which persist much of the time. The strength of this current of air, which encircles the globe, varies with the season and with the general storm systems. Because of the rotation of the earth about its axis, an observer on the ground generally sees a movement of the atmosphere from the west toward the east. The atmosphere as a whole is always moving west to east. At heights of 20,000–40,000 ft above the ground, aircraft at times encounter, in addition to the general westerly flow, very strong currents of air which are referred to as the jet stream. These winds of the jet stream are often 100 mph or greater and may flow from varying directions, although they generally flow from the west. When an aircraft flies against them, its ground speed is reduced accordingly.

Near the ground surface, where most of us live, the winds of the world are slowed and stirred into strange patterns, which are much more complex than the general circulation pattern high above. Air is a viscous fluid, not as viscous or sticky as molasses, nor even as thick as water, but it does have viscosity which transmits the drag forces of the rough surface into the air above. Therefore the rough, rocky, and vegetated surface of the earth creates a drag on the whirling mass of air, so that near the surface the air movement is slowed considerably and is even reversed in direction, as great eddies or *cyclones* (horizontal circular movements of air) are created. Although the general trend is for the air to flow from west to east near the surface, often, at a given place, the winds will come from east, north, or south, or in fact from any direction of the compass. The enormous slowing down of the air movement near the ground permits us to live in relative comfort much of the time, but our gratitude for this should be to the features which roughen the surface of our planet.

The direction of the wind at a particular locale is a definitive measure of the weather conditions of the moment and is a good indicator of conditions to come. Usually any shift in the wind, from prevailing westerlies, implies some sort of a storm disturbance in the region. A south wind may bring warm, moist air and increasing cloudiness; a northwest wind may bring clearing weather and sweep pollutants out of the air. Some of the old proverbs tell best the story of wind.

When the wind backs and the weather glass falls
Then be on your guard against gales and squalls.

or

The wind from the north-east,
Neither good for man nor beast
The wind in the west
Suits everyone best.

or

The winds of the daytime wrestle and fight
Longer and stronger than those of the night.

Calm air is considered as air movement less than 1 mph. Light air movement is 1-3 mph, a light breeze 4-7 mph, a gentle breeze 8-12 mph, a moderate breeze 13-18 mph, a fresh breeze 19-24 mph, a strong breeze 25-31 mph, gale winds 32-63 mph, storm winds 64-73 mph, and winds greater than 74 mph are considered to be of hurricane intensity. Most days our winds are within the breeze category and usually less than 5 mph. The air movement that you experience depends primarily on where you live. Coastal areas are windier than most forested inland regions, grasslands, or deserts. Well-watered regions tend to be less turbulent, while mountain tops are persistently windy locales, even when tree-covered. Windy regions of the world are somewhat more irritating and disagreeable to man, but people do settle in them and learn to live with the winds. High winds of gale proportions can damage some man-made structures and may break an occasional tree limb. Usually around vegetation air movement is low, and at the soil surface, where most animals live, the air is nearly still. This affords protection to wildlife and allows plants to root securely. Only the most intense winds, associated with hurricanes or tornadoes, will disrupt these habitats.

Winds can be devastating. Hurricanes occur in North America and typhoons occur in the Pacific Ocean region. Thunderstorms are frequent in continental climates, but extreme situations along squall lines spawn tornadoes. The twister, which is natural but of enormous destructive force, occurs in violent frontal situations. Tornadoes occur over much of the United States but are far more prevalent within some of the central states. A Kansas farmer, Will Keller, once described how a tornado looked to him:

At last the great shaggy end of the funnel hung directly overhead. Everything was as still as death. There was a strong gassy odor and it seemed that I could not breathe. There was a screaming, hissing sound coming directly from the end of the funnel. I looked up and to my astonishment I saw right up into the heart of the tornado. There was a circular opening in the center of the funnel, about 50 or 100 feet in diameter, and extending straight upward for a distance of at least one half mile, as best as I could judge under the circumstances. The walls of this opening were of rotating clouds and the whole was made brilliantly visible by constant flashes of lightning which zigzagged from side to side. Had it not been for the lightning I could not have seen the opening, not any distance up into it anyway.

Around the lower rim of the great vortex small tornadoes were constantly forming and breaking way. These looked like tails as they writhed their way around the end of the funnel. It was these that made the hissing sound. . . .

The tornado was not traveling at a great speed. I had plenty of time to get a good view of the whole thing, inside and out. . . . Its course was not in a straight line, but it zigzagged across the country, in a general northeasterly direction.

After it passed my place it again dipped and struck and demolished the house and barn of a farmer by the name of Evans. The Evans family, like ourselves, had been looking over their hailed-out wheat and saw the tornado coming. Not having time to reach their cellar they took refuge under a small bluff that faced to the leeward of the approaching tornado. They lay down flat on the ground and caught hold of some plum bushes which fortunately grew within their reach. As it was, they felt themselves lifted from the ground. Mr. Evans said that he could see the wreckage of his house, among it being the cook stove, going round and round over his head. The eldest child, a girl of 17, being the most exposed, had her clothing completely torn off. But none of the family were hurt. . . .*

The funnel cloud of a tornado moves across country at 30–40 mph in a northeasterly direction. The length of path averages about 10 miles. A great deal of electrical activity is associated with the center of a tornado funnel. In fact one hypothesis insists that much of the vortex structure and strong winds are associated with the electrical activity. Wind speeds within the tornado may reach 300 mph or more. Concrete, steel-reinforced buildings are twisted and torn apart by tornadoes. Wooden houses may be totally demolished to kindling and spread across the countryside. In the devastating tornado of June 1966 which struck Topeka, Kansas, automobiles were picked up and dropped into buildings whose roofs had been torn off. The tornado cut a swath across Topeka nearly five miles long and several blocks wide. The path of destruction looked like the aftermath of a major battle. All large trees

*Will Keller, *Monthly Weather Review*, National Weather Service, Washington, D.C., May 1930.

were stripped of leaves, branches were broken, and trunks were splintered. Houses and buildings were either totally destroyed or gutted by the force of the winds.

Many communities have installed tornado warning systems. Usually an air raid siren is sounded if tornadoes are likely to occur in the vicinity. Periods of tornado alerts are broadcast on radio and television. The fact that tornadoes have intense electrical activity associated with them has led Newton Weller of Ames, Iowa, to reason that the electromagnetic waves, or *sferics*, which are generated by the electrical discharges, would, if detectable, be suitable as a warning system. Investigators had found that sferics occurring at a rate of 10–100 per second at a radio frequency of about 150 kHz (kilohertz) were associated with tornadoes. Mr. Weller discovered that the 54–60 kHz components of the sferic would brighten a television screen for periods of several minutes. From this observation he devised the following scheme for tornado detection: (1) Warm up your television as for viewing, but with the contrast control turned to maximum; (2) turn the dial to Channel 13, or to your highest numbered channel; (3) by adjusting the brightness of the picture, or blank screen, reduce the contrast to the threshold of black; (4) and then turn the selector to Channel 2, but do not reset the brightness. Lightning appears on the screen as flashes. If the screen becomes bright or the darkened picture now becomes visible, this is the signal of a tornado within about 20 miles or less. The method is very useful but should be used in conjunction with the official weather bureau forecast of ESSA (Environmental Science Services Administration), which has recently been made part of the N.O.A.A. (National Oceanic and Atmospheric Administration). The absence of a response by the Weller method cannot be guaranteed to be a sign of safety, but its presence calls for added precaution.

The most devastating storm ever to strike the mainland of the United States was hurricane Camille, which dealt death and destruction from 14 to 22 August 1969 along the coast of Mississippi and inland to Virginia. Winds near Camille's eye were estimated to exceed 190 mph. Damage exceeded $1.42 billion, and there were 255 persons killed. Hurricane Camille was small in size with hurricane-force winds extending only to about 45 miles in radius. Hurricane Betsy in 1965 wreaked $1.42 billion damage, but there were many fewer deaths. The giant hurricane Carla in 1961 spread sustained hurricane-force winds from Corpus Christi to Galveston, Texas, a distance of 180 miles. The Galveston hurricane of 1900 killed 6000 people. Atmospheric pressure within a large hurricane will drop to 27.20–27.40 inches of mercury. These storms will raise tides along the Gulf Coast from 5 to 20 ft or more and bring rains as great as 30–40 in. Hurricanes are given the names of ladies even though their behavior is anything but ladylike. The name is retired from use if the storm is of devastating proportions, a dubious distinction indeed.

moisture

Water in our world environment is truly ubiquitous—it is everywhere. Water is a part of all living things. Water is in the skies above us as vapor, clouds, and precipitation, in the form of rain, mist, dew, snow, sleet, or hail. Water is underground, freely moving among strata of rock, or bound within the soil to move from particle to particle by diffusion. Ponds, lakes, seas, oceans, rivers, and streams are reservoirs of water which wash the global surface and shape the character of climates. Without water there would be no life, and our landscape would resemble the harsh environment of the moon or Mars.

A parcel of air can contain only a specific maximum amount of water before it will condense out. How much water vapor the air parcel can hold depends upon the temperature and pressure of the air. When the air contains the maximum amount of water vapor it is said to be saturated and to have a relative humidity of 100%. Air containing less than the saturated amount is described as having a relative humidity less than 100%. Absolutely dry air has a relative humidity of 0%. The very driest climates on earth may have relative humidities at times between 5% and 10%, but, more commonly, dry regions have relative humidities between 10% and 30%. Moist regions of the world have relative humidities from 60% to 80%, and when it is raining, or when there is fog, the relative humidity is 100%. Very clean air without condensation nuclei can be supersaturated and at times exceed 100% relative humidity. When a parcel of air with a certain water vapor content is warmed, the relative humidity will drop, and if it is cooled, the relative humidity will increase. Hence, when you draw cool moist air in winter from outdoors into your home and warm it with your furnace, there results a substantial reduction in its relative humidity. For this reason most of our homes in the winter now have air which is undesirably dry. Such dry air not only tends to dry out your nasal passages and skin, but it also makes it difficult for some household plants to grow.

Precipitation is generally measured in terms of centimeters or inches of liquid water on a horizontal surface. The equivalent amount of water contained in snowfall is measured in terms of its liquid water content if it were melted. The water content of snow varies enormously. Often it requires 8–10 in. of snow depth to produce 1 in. of liquid water. Annual amounts of precipitation vary from the driest in the world, such as in parts of the Sahara and Chile, where only 1 or 2 mm (millimeters) or less are recorded, to the wettest regions, such as Cherrapunji, India, with an annual average rainfall of 1080 cm or 426 in. At the same station in India more than 610 cm or 241 in. of rain fell in one month. The maximum rainfall recorded for a 24-h (hour) period was at Baguio on the island of Luzon in the Philippines, where 117 cm, or 46 in., was measured. This is equivalent to nearly 4 ft of rain on a horizontal surface in a single 24-h period. Such rainfall is a demonstration of the enormous precipitation which can occur in a mountain region, when moist air from a warm ocean cools rapidly, as it rises over the colder mountain slopes. The average annual precipitation for the United States is approximately 76.2 cm or 30 in.

Dew is a significant form of precipitation and usually forms when other precipitation is least likely.

When the dew is on the grass,
Rain will never come to pass.
When grass is dry at morning light,
Look for rain before the night.

Dew is the condensation of moisture onto the ground surface
and on and around vegetation, as the result of the surface
being cooler than the air, which is saturated with moisture.
Several millimeters of dew may condense during the night, and
in many localities this is an important source of moisture for
plants. Along the northwest coast of the United States much
fog precipitation, in the form of dew, is responsible for the
abundant growth of the giant redwoods and the Douglas fir.
Fog is an important feature of many climates and is, of course,
a great deterrent to airplane transportation. Great effort is
being made to develop methods of cloud seeding and of fog
dispersal.

Fog from seaward, weather fair;
Fog from land brings rainy air.

Hail is a destructive form of precipitation which causes millions of dollars of damage to crops and property annually.
Hail occurs most frequently in regions where large thunderstorms build to great heights. This allows the ice particles,
being formed within the storm, to rise and fall many times between the freezing zones and the wet regions of the cloud, until a mass forms of sufficient size to drop out of the cloud as a
hailstone. Much research is being done in Italy, the Soviet
Union, and the United States on hail suppression. These are
countries where hail damage to crops is particularly heavy.
Cloud-seeding techniques are used in an attempt to get the hail
to fall out of the cloud as relatively small particles, rather than
allowing the buildup of large hailstones.

Snow is an important form of precipitation, which blankets
cold regions of the earth during particular times of the year.
Ice and snow formation in cold, moist air requires the presence
of nuclei of dust or dirt for freezing to occur. Pure water

droplets can be cooled to about $-40°C$ before spontaneous ice formation will take place. Snow consists of hexagonal crystals of ice, which are branched and often star-shaped; the exact form of the ice crystals depends upon the temperature of the cloud where freezing occurs. If freezing occurs at temperatures from $0°C$ ($32°F$) down to $-3°C$ ($26.6°F$), hexagonal plates of ice will form; down to $-5°C$ ($23°F$) needles; to $-8°C$ ($17.6°F$) hollow prismatic columns; to $-12°C$ ($10.4°F$) hexagonal plates; to $-16°C$ ($3.2°F$) dendritic, fernlike crystals; to $-25°C$ ($-13°F$) hexagonal plates; and below this temperature the crystals will be hollow prisms. A person in a snowstorm can observe the form of the crystals falling on his jacket and estimate the temperature of the cloud where the crystals are being formed.

Enormous snowfalls may occur in mountainous regions and near lakes. Single storms can dump as much as 1 m (meter) of snow on some areas. Average annual snowfall in some areas exceeds 2.5 m, and maximum annual amounts may exceed 5.0 m in the Rocky Mountains, Cascades, and Sierras. The climate within and beneath a blanket of snow is very favorable to many plants and animals. Often the temperatures are only slightly below the freezing level, and many plants and animals are protected from the intense cold and wind above the snow. Lemmings, shrews, and other mammals tunnel and live comfortably at the ground–snow interface.

Lakes, particularly large ones, such as the Great Lakes, affect the amount of snowfall over land downwind from the lake. Throughout the autumn and winter the lake is a source of heat. Cold air passing over the lake picks up heat and moisture, creating instability and a general increase in cloudiness and precipitation. When this air mass flows over the land downwind from the lake, it cools and dumps much of the moisture as snow. Downwind from Lake Erie, from Buffalo to Schenectady, there is a snow belt where greatly increased amounts of snow fall during winter and spring. In Michigan, along the eastern shoreline of Lake Michigan, at least 30% of the snowfall during the seasons 1957–1958 and 1961–1962 was the result of the lake's influence. Evidence indicates that the lake's effect has increased significantly during the past several decades, particularly in southwestern Michigan and northern Indiana. It seems likely that a general cooling of winter temperatures is partially responsible for the climate change. During the spring and summer months the lake acts like a heat sink and restricts the development of convective cloudiness and precipitation along the shoreline. During summers the coastal areas downwind of the lake should be sunny and suitable for resorts.

surface effects

There are great variations of air temperature, moisture, and wind in the space near the ground. The vertical profiles of temperature, moisture, and wind depend very much on the nature of the terrain. If the surface is forested, then within the forest these factors may change very slowly, and only above and beyond the forest are the changes very large. Near the ground and in the open, the variation with time and temperature, wind, and moisture is sometimes very great, both in the daytime and at night. When the sun is striking an exposed soil surface it may cause the surface to have a temperature as much as $30°C$ above the air temperature at a height of 1 m. During midday the sunlit soil surface temperature is normally at a higher temperature than the soil beneath the surface. At a depth of 1 m or more the temperature is nearly constant day and night. Vast numbers of plants and animals live at or close to the soil–air interface, and these enormous gradients of temperature are uniquely characteristic of their microclimate. The air near the soil surface may be humid, particularly if the soil is saturated with moisture, and yet it may be quite dry a meter or so above the surface. At night, especially when the sky is clear, the soil surface becomes very cool due to radiational cooling. The temperature of the soil surface may drop $10°C$ $(18°F)$ below the air temperature by the early morning hours. As the air temperature drops, the relative humidity will rise. Those organisms living at the soil–air interface, such as plants, bacteria, spores, and others which cannot move and escape the surface, may experience a temperature change from

5°C (9°F) at night to 60°C (140°F) in the daytime, although the air temperature may vary only between 15°C (41°F) at night and 35°C (95°F) during the day. These great extremes of environmental temperatures at the soil surface may be of considerable significance in the evolution of organisms adapted to these habitats.

It takes time for heat to penetrate a substance to a given depth. Generally speaking, it takes 1 h for heat to penetrate soil 3.1 cm or 32 h to penetrate 1 m. It is clear that the daily cycle of heating and cooling is effective only within about 75 cm of the soil surface.

The change of wind speed from a few meters above the ground, as one approaches the surface, is very striking. A wind of 440 cm sec^{-1} (10 mph) may blow at a height of 2 m. At a height of 10 cm the wind speed may be 44 cm sec^{-1} (1 mph), and it may be nearly zero within a few centimeters of the surface. The reason for this dramatic reduction of wind speed as one approaches the surface is the frictional effect of the surface on the air flow. Because it is a fluid which has a small but definite viscosity, air very close to the surface is strongly retarded by viscous drag, and this retardation is transmitted to the air above with diminishing effect. Since there is usually very little wind in the boundary layer close to the ground surface, the environment here is generally the hottest during the day with the least convectional cooling, and it is the coolest during the night with the least convectional warming.

climate comparisons

From the weather over a period of years emerge the climates of regions, fields, woods, hills, and valleys, where man must live. The earth is an unusual planet among the satellites of the sun. It is at just the right distance from the sun in order not to be too hot or too cold, but to receive the proper amount of radiant heat for life to thrive. Vegetation and the atmosphere have evolved together in synergism, and a delicate balance exists between them. The atmosphere is a giant "filter" and at the same time it is our "window" into space. It screens out ultraviolet and infrared rays but passes on an abundance of sunlight which plants use for photosynthesis. The long-wave infrared heat radiation emitted by the ground is partially trapped by the atmosphere, and some of the warmth is returned to the surface. By letting in just the right amount of sunlight and by not allowing too much heat to escape, the atmosphere protects the green surface against the intense destructive rays of the sun and against the cosmic cold of outer space. Nevertheless, conditions on earth are highly variable as to the amount of radiation received, the temperature, and the quantities of moisture and wind present. The poles are dark and cold all winter, and they are sunlit and warmer all summer. The tropics receive nearly uniform quantities of radiation, summer and winter, and the temperatures of air and soil tend toward uniformity throughout the year. In the middle latitudes of the planet the so-called temperate regions of the world are anything but temperate. The greatest extremes of rainfall, temperature change, and wind usually occur within the mid-latitude continental regions. Climates of mountains are particularly variable, and they usually have a wet side and a dry side, depending upon the direction of the prevailing winds.

Radiation, air temperature, wind, and moisture are the parameters we use to describe the weather and the climate. The ground surface of the earth is highly irregular. The climate of any region, or of any particular place on earth, is very much a function of the contour of the surface. North-facing or south-facing slopes within the same valley have entirely different climates, as does the hilltop and the valley bottom. The open meadow, forest interior, sand dune surface, lake shore, and urban area have strikingly different climates. It is necessary that we have a basis for comparison and discussion of these various climates. It is best if we can make some sort of a quantitative comparison of climates, but even descriptive classifications are useful.

3

climate classification

There is no topic discussed more frequently by people everywhere than the weather and the local climate. Our lives are affected in every way by climate. It determines whether or not we heat or cool our homes, the manner of construction of our houses, how much and what kind of clothing we wear, whether or not our transportation system functions properly, how operable are our communications, how much food is produced, and whether or not we are healthy or ill. Each person classifies the climate of his part of the country or makes a subjective comparison of his climate with the climate elsewhere. There is often little agreement among various people as to whether or not the climate of their region is good or bad. The variation in judgment depends upon attitude, past experience, and one's own physiological comfort or desire for certain kinds of conditions.

When we speak of a climate as good or bad, or better or worse, just what do we mean? Good or bad for what? Is the climate good or bad for plants, for animals, for people, or specifically for corn or for alligators? In essence there is no such thing as a bad or good climate, but only climates with various characteristics.

*climate
classification*

The Eskimos like the climate along the fringe of the Arctic Ocean, and the nomads of the Sahara like the desert climate. Many millions of people in the modern world are adapting to the climates of cities and feel uncomfortable when removed from the protection of buildings, concrete surfaces, and the many people around them all the time. Man judges a climate according to his past experience, to his likes and dislikes, to his conditioning, and even as a result of his evolutionary genetic history and selection.

It becomes apparent that we should attempt an objective classification of climate. In fact, a classification scheme to be generally useful should be as quantitative as possible. But what is the purpose for climate classification? Is it for the purpose of growing plants, for the comfort of people, for the production of livestock, or for some other reason? Actually, the climate classification of a particular region should involve only the physical parameters of the weather averaged over periods of time. It might be that the native vegetation of the region is a good indicator of the type of climate which prevails there, or the livestock production may reflect certain favorable or unfavorable factors, but the climate is a characteristic of the weather averaged over a season, or a portion of a season, using information collected from as many years as possible. Usually we speak of the climate of a clearly defined geographical region, e.g., the climate of Massachusetts or Kansas, of northern Michigan, eastern Colorado, or northern California. We can describe the climate of smaller geographic units, such as a mountain valley, the Los Angeles basin, the Mississippi delta, or the Everglades. When we describe the climate of very small areas, for example, the climate of our lawn, or of the interior of a forest, or of a building for that matter, we are describing microclimates, sometimes called "climates in miniature" or the "climate near the ground." We are concerned here with both climates and microclimates, for each is of sufficient import to merit much discussion.

Hinds's climate types

The first attempt at a semiquantitative classification of climate in modern times was made by a young British scientist, Richard Brinsley Hinds, assistant surgeon on HMS Sulphur during an extensive voyage of the Pacific Ocean between 1835 and 1842. Hinds's first note on climate was submitted to the *Magazine of Natural History* in 1835 just as the HMS Sulphur was departing England. Subsequent papers were published in 1842 just prior to, and at the time of, his return to England. Apparently Hinds had sent some of his manuscripts home by faster ships than the Sulphur. Hinds's interest in climate was directly related to his interest in plant and animal distribution throughout the world. An example of the climate classification by Hinds is given in Table 1.

The climate classification system of Hinds takes into account the major weather factors, i.e., temperature and moisture. Wind and radiation are omitted, but they are of less importance. However, Hinds cleverly adds another factor to his classification and that is the time variability, or the stability, of

table 1
climate classification of the world by Richard Hinds

mean temperature 70–84°F

Hot and dry, seasons in extremes
Hot and dry, seasons even, e.g., Arabia
Hot and moist, seasons in extremes, e.g., China
Hot and moist, seasons even, e.g., Malay Islands

mean temperature 55–70°F

Warm and dry, seasons in extremes, e.g., Asia Minor
Warm and dry, seasons even, e.g., Egypt
Warm and moist, seasons in extremes, e.g., southern U.S.
Warm and moist, seasons even, e.g., Canary Islands

mean temperature 45–55°F

Temperate and dry, seasons in extremes
Temperate and dry, seasons even
Temperate and moist, seasons in extremes
Temperate and moist, seasons even, e.g., England

mean temperature 32–45°F

Cold and dry, seasons in extremes, e.g., Canada
Cold and dry, seasons even
Cold and moist, seasons in extremes, e.g., Siberia
Cold and moist, seasons even, e.g., North of Scotland

Source: Arnold Court, Weather **22**, No. 7, July (1967), p. 277.

the climate. He did not assign quantitative values to the variability or to the precipitation, but he clearly used values in his judgment concerning the climate of a particular place. After all it was 1840 when Hinds devised his climate classification.

Climatologists of the nineteenth century recognized that the vegetation types of the world reflected the climate of the region by their manner of growth. The plants respond to the amount of water available, the hours of sunshine, the temperatures of the region, and the wind. The plants integrate all of these weather factors into their response. Whether a region is prairie, chapparal, forest, desert, or tundra is a direct result of the climate, the soil type, and the particular plant species which are available in that part of the world. But the soil type, for instance, results from the interaction of the parent rock material with the plants and with the climate. What we are really saying is that the physiognomic character of an area is not the result of one of these factors alone, but each is interlocked with the other, and all interact to form the landscape character, including the climate, of the region. Hence, when vegetation units were used to help classify climates of the world, they were looked upon as indicators.

Köppen's climate types

The botanist De Candolle established a system of climate classification during the nineteenth century which was strongly based on types of plant communities. The first modern attempt at classification of climates was by the German climatologist Wladimir Köppen, who lived a very long and productive life. He published his system in 1918 and revised it in 1923. Köppen's first division of climates was into five groups as follows:

A   Tropical rainy climates
B   Dry climates
C   Warm temperate rainy climates
D   Cold snow forest climates
E   Polar climates

Trees will grow only in climates *A*, *C*, and *D*, since the *B* and *E* climates are too dry and too cold respectively. Köppen followed the suggestion of earlier workers in defining the lower limit for hot climates as 20°C (68°F) for the mean annual air temperature and 10°C (50°F) as the upper limit for the warmest month for polar zones. Actually for trees to get through their reproductive cycle they need three months at maximum temperatures above 6°C (43°F).

Köppen subdivided his five main climate classes into a total of eleven climate provinces. Attempts were made to subdivide the Köppen classification system further, but it became unwieldy. Furthermore, the symbols used refer to the German language, and it is difficult for English-speaking people to remember the classification. The eleven climate provinces are given in Table 2.

Within the United States only Florida has a tropical climate *A*, with an average temperature during the coldest month greater than 18°C (65°F) and with a winter dry season *Aw*, and that is in the Everglades and the tip of southern Florida. Usually the steppe *BS* and desert *BW* climates are found along the west coasts of land areas in the subtropics, but these climates are found also in the United States in the rain shadow to the east of the Sierra Nevadas and to the east of the Rocky Mountains, e.g., the Great Basin, Sonoran and Mojave deserts, and the high plains. Temperate climate *Cf* is found along most of the east coast of the United States and inland through the Midwest to the high plains and south of the southern border of Iowa. Temperate climate *Cs* is found mostly along the west coast, and cold, humid climate *Df*, with no dry period, is found throughout the upper Midwest, east of the high plains. There are localized areas of tundra climate *ET* on the tops of the Rockies and Sierras.

Thornthwaite's climate types

Köppen's system of climate classification is used in many books and atlases throughout most countries of the world. Yet the system has severe limitations, in that it is based primarily on temperature and does not agree with the vegetation types

table 2

type of climates as classified by Köppen

main type	climate province	symbol	temperature	rainfall	vegetation
Tropical rain	Rain forest	Af	Coldest month > 18°C Annual variation < 3°C	Heavy rain Min. 6 cm/month	Dense forest; heavy undergrowth
	Savanna	Aw	Coldest month > 18°C Annual variation < 12°C	Dry season with < 6 cm/month	Open grasslands; scattered trees
Dry	Steppe	BS	Variable winters cold	Rain < 50 cm/year	Short grass
	Desert	BW	High summer temp.	Very dry	Sparse or none
Warm, humid (Temperate)	Mediterranean	Cf	Coldest month between 18°C and -3°C Warmest month > 10°C	Ample rain throughout year	Cotton, wheat, and corn
	Winter dry	Cw	Coldest month between 18°C and -3°C Warmest month > 10°C	Wet summer	Forest
	Summer dry	Cs		Dry summer	
Cold, humid	Cold with no dry period	Df	Mean temp. of summer is 10°C, of winter -3°C	Rain even throughout year	Canada
	Dry winter	Dw			N.E. Asia only
Polar	Tundra	ET	Mean temp. of warmest month < 10°C	Frozen soil	Moss and small shrubs
	Ice cap	EF	Mean temp. of warmest month < 0°C		

found in certain regions of the world. Clearly something was not properly included. C. Warren Thornthwaite, following the ecologist Transeau and others, came up with a formula to express numerically a precipitation-effectiveness index, based on the sum for the year of the precipitation-evaporation ratios P/E. The mean monthly precipitation P is divided by the mean monthly evaporation E of a free water surface in a pan to give the monthly P/E ratio from which the so-called precipitation-effectiveness index (P-E index) is calculated for the year as follows:

$$P\text{-}E \text{ index} = \sum_{n=1}^{12} 10 \left(\frac{P}{E}\right)_n \tag{1}$$

Thornthwaite recognized that often pan evaporation data were not available from certain stations and devised a formula based on mean monthly precipitation P and mean monthly temperature T which would agree reasonably well with that using evaporation. This formula is as follows:

$$P\text{-}E \text{ index} = \sum_{n=1}^{12} 115 \left(\frac{P}{T-10}\right)_n^{10/9} \tag{2}$$

Perhaps this is a bit awkward to calculate since each monthly $P/(T-10)$ ratio must be taken to the $\frac{10}{9}$th power before all the twelve monthly values are added together and multiplied by 115, yet it is useful. Thornthwaite warns that it does not apply with accuracy to mean monthly temperatures below $30°$F and above $90°$F.

The Thornthwaite precipitation-effectiveness indices are given in Table 3. Because of the roughly cyclic character of the annual progression of temperature and precipitation and the seasonal variations of the P/E ratios, Thornthwaite found it necessary to distinguish between the seasonably dry and the continuously dry areas, and he established the following four subtypes: r = abundance of moisture at all seasons; s = mois-

table 3
humidity provinces of Thornthwaite

humidity province	characteristic vegetation	P-E index
A Wet	Rain forest	128 and above
B Humid	Forest	64–127
C Subhumid	Grassland	32–63
D Semiarid	Steppe	16–31
E Arid	Desert	less than 16

Source: C. Warren Thornthwaite, Geograph. Rev. **21**, Oct. (1931), p. 641.

ture deficient in the summer; w = moisture deficient in the winter; and d = moisture deficient at all seasons of the year.

Thornthwaite found that where thermal, edaphic, and cultural conditions are constant there is a direct relation between the amount of vegetation on an area and the P-E index of the area. The lower the P-E index the less favorable is the area for growth of vegetation. Aridity is a limiting factor for plant growth. It has been found that where moisture is adequate, plant growth is proportional to temperature. Cold temperatures are limiting to plant growth just as seriously as lack of water is limiting. Very high temperatures can be limiting also. Thornthwaite developed a temperature index which would include the growth-limiting effect of low temperatures and the stimulating influence of warmer temperatures without getting into the higher temperature limitations. He devised a monthly coefficient of temperature efficiency called the T/E ratio and by summing the monthly values on an annual basis derived a T-E index as follows:

$$T\text{-}E \text{ index} = \sum_{n=1}^{12} \left(\frac{T-32}{4}\right)_n \tag{3}$$

where T is the mean monthly temperature for a station. Six temperature provinces were defined as shown in Table 4.

Just as with the P-E index it was necessary to take into account the seasonal variation of precipitation, with the T-E index one must recognize that much of the warmth for the

table 4
temperature provinces of Thornthwaite

temperature province	T-E index
A' Tropical	128 and above
B' Temperate	64–127
C' Cold	32–63
D' Taiga	16–31
E' Tundra	1–15
F' Frost	0

Source: C. Warren Thornthwaite, Geograph.
Rev. **21**, Oct. (1931), p. 646.

year may be concentrated during the summer months. The summer, which is the warmest period of the year, cannot contribute less than 25% of the total annual heat accumulation under any circumstances. At the other extreme, it might contribute nearly 100% of the total. Thornthwaite defined five subprovinces of temperature efficiency as follows: a = 25-34% summer contribution; b = 35-49%; c = 50-69%; d = 70-99%; e = 100%. The index of summer concentration varies with latitude and with distance from the ocean.

Now the P-E index and the T-E index can both be used to describe the climate of an area in terms of its influence on plant growth. Since so much depends upon vegetation—the character of the landscape, the birds and animals of an area, the crop and livestock production, etc.—it becomes of paramount importance to describe accurately the climate of a region in terms of the potential vegetation growth. Where temperature efficiency is adequate, the precipitation effectiveness may limit vegetation climate boundaries. On the other hand, where precipitation is adequate, temperature efficiency may determine the climate boundaries. If the T-E index for a region is less than 32, it controls the climate; if the index is more than 32, the climate is controlled by precipitation effectiveness. If temperature efficiency is limiting, T-E index < 32, then the climate is D', E' or F'. If temperature efficiency is adequate, T-E index > 32, then the P-E effectiveness classes will always have A', B', or C' appended to them as follows: AA', AB', AC'; BA', BB', BC'; CA', CB', CC'; DA', DB', DC';

EA', EB', EC'. The subtypes for precipitation effectiveness will group as follows: $A(r$ only); $B(r, s,$ or $w)$; $C(r, s, w,$ or $d)$; $D(s, w,$ or $d)$; and $E(d$ only). Actually in the A' subdivisions of B, C, and D the summer dry (s) subtype never occurs.

The climates of North America, according to the Thornthwaite classification, are mapped in Fig. 9. The various types of climate found on the North American continent are discussed in the following paragraphs.

The A climates are found as $AA'ra$ in Mexico on the Gulf of Campeche and partly in Vera Chiapas to the south of Tobasco.

figure 9. *The climates of North America according to Thornthwaite's classification.*

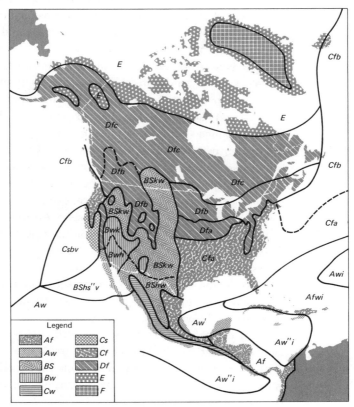

$AB'ra$ and $AB'rb$ (wet, temperate, with moisture throughout the year and summer temperatures only 25-34% and 35-49% of the year, respectively) are extremely limited in a small section of the northwest coast of California, a little in the interior, and a small amount in the Blue Ridge Mountains of western South Carolina and northern Georgia. $AC'rb$ and $AC'rc$ (wet, cold, with moisture throughout the year, and summer temperatures only 35-49% and 50-69% of the total year, respectively) are found along the west coast of northern California up to Sitka in Alaska, the west-facing slopes of the Coast Ranges, and sometimes in the Appalachian Mountains, the Catskills, and the Adirondacks.

The B climates are few in Mexico, but the eastern United States and southeastern Canada have almost entirely B climates. The southern tip of Florida is $BA'ra$ (humid, tropical, even moisture throughout the year and 25-34% summer season temperature accrual). $BB'ra$ (humid, temperate, even, and 25-34% summer temperature) is along the coast of the Gulf of Mexico in eastern Texas, Louisiana, Mississippi, Alabama, Florida, and Georgia. $BB'rb$ (humid, temperate, even, and 35-49% summer temperature) includes the entire area from the eastern parts of Texas, Oklahoma, and Kansas to the Atlantic coast and north to Iowa and central Illinois. The northern portion of the United States and the southern portion of eastern Canada are $BC'rc$ (humid, cool, even, and 50-69% temperature accrual in summer). In western America the B climates are much less extensive than in the east. From central California northward into British Columbia and eastward across the Cascades and Sierras the regions not in the A category are in the B class. As one proceeds upward within any mountain range the climate types change. Certain high elevation areas in the western states are $BC'rc$.

The C climates are most finely divided. Running from the Gulf of Mexico north through the central United States into Canada are two parallel belts of C climates, the eastern belt, where rainfall is always sufficient, and the western belt, where rainfall is limiting. Through Texas, Oklahoma, and Kansas the climates are $CB'rb$ and $CB'db$ (subhumid, temperate, even, and

35-49% temperature accrual in summer or subhumid, temperate, moisture deficient at all seasons, and 35-49% summer temperature, respectively). In the western United States the most extensive C climates are those with a dry summer season. The Mediterranean climate is found in California and is divided by Thornthwaite into $CB'sa$ and $CB'sb$ (subhumid, temperate, dry summer, and 25-34% or 35-49% summer temperature accrual, respectively), which corresponds to Köppen's Csa and Csb climates. There are a number of small areas throughout the Rocky Mountains where C climates prevail. There are C climates in Mexico, which have primarily deficient moisture in the winter, and in Canada with a dry phase deficient in moisture throughout the year.

In western North America the D (semiarid) climates occupy more area than any other climate. East of the Rockies a belt of D climates extends 300-600 miles wide from near Mexico City through the United States and up into Saskatchewan and Alberta. In Kansas and southeastern Colorado the climate is $DB'db$ (semiarid, temperate, dry throughout the year, and 35-49% summer accrual of temperature effects). The San Joaquin Valley of California has a $DB'db$ climate, and the coast of southern California south of Los Angeles has a $DB'da$ climate.

Only two extensive desert areas with E climates are found in North America. One includes parts of northern Mexico, some of Texas, New Mexico, and Arizona, extending up the Rio Grande beyond Albuquerque. The second large desert region includes both coasts of the Gulf of California with most of Baja California on the west and about half of Sonora on the east. Included in this are the southwestern third of Arizona, the eastern part of California, and about half of Nevada.

It is only in the very far north, in the interior of Greenland and over a part of Ellesmere Island, where the F' climate exists. The tundra, or E' climate, includes the Arctic coast and inland as much as 800 miles to the south, as well as the coast of Greenland. The D' climate, represented by the Taiga, comes south nearly to the Canadian border and spreads across Manitoba, Saskatchewan, and Alberta, and north into Alaska to the

Arctic Ocean at Nome, and east to Hudson Bay and Fort Churchill. The D' climate contains more area than any other single climate type in North America.

human climate types

It is interesting that very few have attempted to classify the climates of the world from the human standpoint. Although it might seem that this is less important now that good air conditioners for home, office, and automobile are available, it is still a fact that vast numbers of people have no recourse to these conveniences. We hear the virtues of certain climates extolled by travel agents, but how do they actually know? Seldom has a careful analysis been made to prove that the climate of a particular place is highly suitable for certain human activities at a specfic time of the year. Certainly, in view of the many ways that climatic conditions affect our activities, attitudes, general spirit, and health, it might be interesting to attempt a quantitative formulation of climate. A few years ago W. J. Maunder of the University of Otago at Dunedin, New Zealand, attempted a human classification of climate. I shall present his classification scheme here because I find it interesting and challenging. It is challenging because one wonders how it might be improved upon, and it raises the critical question of just what one means by a favorable or unfavorable climate. It is interesting because one wonders, just how favorable or unfavorable are the climates of various parts of our country?

We might disagree with Maunder's classification with respect to certain specifics, but it is an interesting beginning on the problem. Certainly to attempt to classify climates from strictly the comfort index standpoint is not satisfactory because often when the degree of discomfort is high the climate is highly satisfactory for some kinds of endeavor. Furthermore the comfort index does not take into account duration of sunshine, rain, wind, and degrees of warmth or cold. A comparison of climates must be made on a complete annual basis and must include some consideration of winter and summer conditions separately, as well as the annual mean conditions. A certain climate may be highly satisfactory part of the year and simply wretched another part of the year. In some way all of this must be taken into consideration, and this is what Maunder has attempted.

The factors used in Maunder's formula for evaluating a human climate index X are listed in Table 5 along with the range of values for each rating from 1, for most favorable, to 5, for least favorable. There are three rainfall factors to take into consideration, two sunshine factors, five temperature factors, one humidity measure, and two measures of windiness. The various factors are weighted according to Maunder's judgment of their relative importance. The human climate index is evaluated as follows:

$$X = (3R_1 + 3R_2 + 2R_3) + (4S_1 + 3S_2)$$
$$+ (2T_1 + T_2 + T_3 + T_4 + T_5) + (5H_1) + (2W_1 + 2W_2)$$
$$(4)$$

Winter is taken to be the three months December, January, and February in the Northern Hemisphere and June, July, and August in the Southern Hemisphere. Days with *screen frost* are days when the screen temperature is below 0°C (32°F). The word "screen" refers to the meteorological instrument shelter. Days with *ground frost* are days when the grass minimum temperature is below −0.8°C (30.5°F). For many stations it is going to be difficult to get the information required for the calculation of the human climate index. Often humidity is taken only once a day, as it is at New Zealand stations. Maunder calculated a hypothetical dew point temperature from the mean annual relative humidity and the mean annual maximum daily temperature for the year.

The student should try to get from the local ESSA station the appropriate data for his locale and attempt an original evaluation of the human climate index. In Table 6 values are given of the various factors and the calculated human climate index for a few selected New Zealand stations, to which Maunder applied his empirical formula. The New Zealand climate is considered to be among the best in the

table 5

rating scheme for evaluation of human climate index

factor	rating	1	2	3	4	5
R_1 = Mean annual rainfall (in.)		10.0–17.7	17.8–31.6	31.7–56.2	56.3–99.9	100.0–177.8
R_2 = Mean annual duration of rainfall (h)		355–446	447–562	563–707	708–891	892–1122
R_3 = Percentage of rainfall occurring at night (9 P.M.–9 A.M.)		53.0–54.9	51.0–52.9	49.0–50.9	47.0–48.9	45.0–46.9
S_1 = Mean annual duration of bright sunshine (h)		2400–2599	2200–2399	2000–2199	1800–1999	1600–1799
S_2 = Mean winter duration of bright sunshine (h)		450–499	400–449	350–399	300–349	250–299
T_1 = Mean annual degree-days (base 60°F)		1000–1349	1350–1905	1906–2630	2631–3630	3631–5011
T_2 = Mean number of days with screen frost per year		0–7.9	8.0–23.9	24.0–47.9	48.0–79.9	80.0–119.9
T_3 = Mean daily maximum temperature of coldest month (°F)		56.0–59.9	52.0–55.9	48.0–51.9	44.0–47.9	40.0–43.9
T_4 = Mean annual maximum temperature (°F)		74.0–77.9	78.0–81.9	82.0–85.9	86.0–89.9	90.0–93.9
T_5 = Mean number of days with ground frost per year		0–14.9	15.0–44.9	45.0–89.9	90.0–149.9	150.0–224.9
H_1 = Humidity index expressed as dew point (°F)		50.0–51.9	52.0–53.9	54.0–55.9	56.0–57.9	58.0–59.9
W_1 = Mean number of days with wind gusts ⩾40 mph per year		0–14.9	15.0–44.9	45.0–89.9	90.0–149.9	150.0–224.9
W_2 = Mean number of days with wind gusts ⩾60 mph per year		0–2.4	2.5–4.9	5.0–12.4	12.5–22.4	22.5–35.0

Source: W. J. Maunder, Weather **17**, No. 1, Jan. (1962), p. 9.

world. In Table 6 we see the worst and the best of one of the best climates in the world.

The human climate index for New Zealand ranges from an index of 60 for the best climate to an index of 101 for the worst. If a locale had the best of all possible climates with a 1 in every category, it would have an index of 30. If, on the other hand, the worst possible climate existed and the rating was 5 in every category, the index would be 150. There are a few locales in the United States which are dry, not too cold in the winter, nor too hot in the summer, and which, with much sunshine throughout the year, would have human climate indices of about 50. There are certainly such places in California, perhaps a place or two in Arizona, and the narrow strip east of the Rocky Mountains in Colorado, including Colorado Springs, Denver, and Boulder. We do not have available the proper data to make an accurate estimate of the human climate index for the United States, but it is something which would be interesting and worthwhile to do.

microclimate classification

The climate surrounding an organism is the climate which is really significant for the comfort, behavior, and viability of the organism. In the last chapter it is shown how climate or microclimate is coupled to an organism by a flow of energy, and that the significant factors are the amount of radiation absorbed by an organism's surface, the air temperature, the wind speed, and the relative humidity. Most classifications of climate have not dealt with the amount of radiation as a ubiquitous, essential property of the environment. Furthermore, most classifications of climate deal with the daily or weekly characteristics as averaged from several years of records. Here I want to describe and classify the microclimate near an organism as it may occur, moment by moment, throughout the day and night.

It is relatively easy for most people to know the air temperatures which are normally encountered and probably to have some realization of the values of relative humidity and wind,

table 6

human climate index for New Zealand

station	R_1	R_2	R_3	S_1	S_2	T_1	T_2	T_3	T_4	T_5	H_1	W_1	W_2	X
Nelson	3	2	2	1	1	3	3	2	3	4	2	2	1	60 Best
Auckland	3	1	4	3	2	1	1	1	2	1	5	3	1	78
Christchurch	2	2	2	4	3	4	3	3	4	4	2	3	2	83
Wellington	3	3	2	3	4	3	1	3	2	2	2	5	5	90
Invercargill	3	3	1	5	5	5	3	3	3	3	2	4	3	101 Worst

Source: W. J. Maunder, Weather **17**, No. 1, Jan. (1962), p. 9.

but very few people have any concept of the quantity of radiation present in the environment in which they live. Although later in this book a more detailed description of the radiation fluxes of our environment is given, it is now necessary to briefly describe the quantities of radiation which we encounter.

All surfaces emit radiation according to the fourth power of their absolute temperature. When one is in a room the radiation emitted by the walls is a definite flux of radiant heat, dependent on the temperature of the walls. If the wall temperature is 10°C (50°F), the amount of radiation emitted is 0.52 cal cm^{-2} min^{-1}, and if the temperature is 20°C (68°F), or 30°C (86°F), it is 0.60 and 0.69 cal cm^{-2} min^{-1}, respectively. At night out of doors and in the open a person receives blackbody radiation from the ground surface according to its temperature and also a lesser amount of radiant heat from a clear sky overhead. If the ground surface is at 0°C (32°F), the quantity of radiation is 0.45 cal cm^{-2} min^{-1}, and the amount from the sky is about 0.25 cal cm^{-2} min^{-1} to give an average flux of 0.35 cal cm^{-2} min^{-1} incident upon a person in that environment. If the sky becomes overcast, then the clouds emit radiation according to the temperature of their base, which might be at -10°C and radiate 0.40 cal cm^{-2} min^{-1} to give an average amount, incident on a person, plant, or animal, of 0.42 cal cm^{-2} min^{-1}. During the daytime the ground radiates according to its surface temperature, but in addition there is a stream of direct solar radiation plus the hemisphere of scattered skylight. Typical values for the fluxes of radiation received by an organism during a warm, clear, sunny summer day are 0.80 from the ground, 0.60 from the atmosphere, 1.20 from the sun directly, and 0.20 from scattered skylight to give an average value between about 1.00 and 1.40 cal cm^{-2} min^{-1}, depending upon the orientation of the organism. The amounts of radiation incident on an organism during an overcast day are somewhat less than these clear day values, but often they are not very much less.

In Table 7 are given the values of radiation for radiation

table 7
classification of microclimates

radiation (cal cm⁻² min⁻¹)	air temperature (°C)	wind (cm sec⁻¹)	humidity (%)
Sunny 1.0–1.6	Hot 30–50	Still 0–50	Dry 0–40
Cloudy 0.6–1.0	Warm 15–30	Breezy 50–200	Humid 40–100
Dark 0–0.6	Temperate 0–15	Windy 200 or more	
	Cold below 0	20	

examples				classification
Sunny	Hot	Still	Dry	SHSD
Sunny	Hot	Still	Humid	SHSH
Sunny	Hot	Breezy	Dry	SHBD
Sunny	Cold	Windy	Humid	SCWH
Cloudy	Cold	Breezy	Humid	CCBH
Cloudy	Hot	Windy	Dry	CHWD
Dark	Cold	Breezy	Dry	DCBD

situations	classification
Field at noon, clear, summer	SHSH
Field at night, cloudy, summer	DWSH
Desert at noon, clear, summer	SHSD
Tree top noon, clear, summer	SHBH
Tree top noon, clear, spring	SWBH
Tree top night, clear, spring	DTSH
Tree top night, cloudy, winter	DCSH
Tree top night, clear, winter	DCWD
Inside forest at noon, summer	CHSH
Inside forest at noon, spring	CWSH
Alpine tundra noon, clear, summer	STVD
Alpine tundra night, cloudy, summer	DCBH
Lake shore noon, cloudy, summer	CWBH
Room in house	CWSD

conditions described as sunny S, cloudy C, and dark D. Similarly, the quantitative limits of air temperature of hot H, warm W, temperate T, and cold C are given; for wind of still S, breezy B, and windy W; and for humidity of dry D and humid H. Using the quantitative limits as specified one can describe various microclimates as shown in Table 7. A sunny, hot, still, dry condition is described as SHSD. From such a description quick reference to the upper part of Table 7 will give the approximate quantitative conditions of this particular microclimate.

It is interesting to classify a few microclimates which are a part of everyday experience or observation. These typical situations are listed in the lower portion of Table 7. A room in which we live would have a microclimate which is classified as CTSD. In this instance the first symbol C does not really imply that the room is cloudy, but rather that it is characterized by the range of values for the radiation flux as specified for a C condition. The room is, of course, temperate in temperature, with relatively still air, and is usually quite dry. The climate of a tree top at noon on a clear day is perhaps SWBH or it might be SHWD, etc.

Consider the climate of a skier in the sun standing still on a snow field at a high altitude in the mountains. The sky is clear, the air is still and cold, $-10°C$ ($14°F$). The relative humidity may be fairly low. The skier's microclimate is SCSD. He is receiving a great deal of radiation, since he gets direct sunlight and skylight, much reflected sunlight from the snow, and, in addition, thermal radiation from the snow surface and nearby pine trees. He becomes so warm because of the energy flowing into his body through his clothing that he takes off his coat. He begins to ski, moving rapidly down the slope. His microclimate is now SCWD, and the convective cooling of the cold air rushing across his surface becomes great; he is chilled and stops to put on his jacket. Soon, however, the sky clouds over, and a storm moves in with an increase of humidity. Standing still on the slope his microclimate is CCSH, but as he skis it is CCWH. His energy budget has changed dramatically, and now the convective cooling is compensated not by high radiation input but by a very low radiation field, since he is sandwiched between a very cold snow surface and a cold cloud surface overhead. Even his snug down-filled jacket may not keep him warm enough. The humidity has increased, and the conductivity of his clothing has increased with the additional moisture. The skier must exercise vigorously, thereby increasing the body heat or metabolic heat, in order to stay warm.

4
climate and man

Man is fragile yet has enormous sustaining power under certain circumstances. Sometimes we think that animals can take much greater climate extremes than man. Only certain animals are hardier to climate than man. Man is clever and devises houses, shelters, and clothing to provide an artifical climate suitable to his thermal needs. Man is an excellent temperature regulator. He maintains his deep body temperature within a few degrees of $37°C$ ($98.6°F$) by varying metabolic rate, perspiration rate, or the quality of thermal insulation by putting on or taking off clothing. The human body is an excellent evaporative cooler when the heat load imposed on it becomes too great for thermal comfort.

Thermal equilibrium is maintained in man by the body's ability to alter its rate of heat production and heat loss. An average-sized, unclothed person at rest can remain in thermal equilibrium in a room with the wall and air temperature at $30°C$ ($86°F$). Under these conditions his minimum heat production by metabolism just balances his heat loss to the room. In any other conditions a man must make physiological adjustments of metabolic rate or of water loss rate, or must put on or take off clothing to remain in thermal equilibrium. Heat loss from the body occurs by radiation, conduction, convection, and the evaporation of water. The relative importance of each varies with the climate conditions. At a room temperature (air and walls) of about 20°C (68°F) man loses about 60% of his heat production by net radiation exchange. At ambient temperatures of 32°C (90°F) the metabolic heat loss is small by radiative exchange and must be accomplished primarily by means of evaporative cooling. Under very cold environmental conditions, say at 0°C (32°F), metabolic heat is lost primarily by radiation and partly by convection in still air. If there is wind, then the convective heat exchange rate increases substantially and the radiation heat loss is reduced.

The nerve center and computer facility for this finely tuned thermal regulation of man is located in the hypothalamus of the anterior region of the brain. Here in the hypothalamus, the primary regulation of body temperature occurs, but there are peripheral temperature sensors throughout the human body which send signals to the brain, where a response by change of metabolic rate, shivering, perspiring, or movement is suggested to the body. Many of the peripheral temperature sensors are located near the skin surface where the temperature is detected and programmed by the brain. Skin surface temperature will vary considerably depending upon external conditions but may range from 33° to 35°C (91.4–95°F) normally. If heat is applied and the skin becomes very warm, as it does when one is standing near a fire or radiator, the threshold for pain is between 44°C and 46°C (111.2–115°F). Man moves away from the source of heat when the skin temperature exceeds this value. When cooled by a cold wind, skin temperatures of exposed parts may go well below 0°C (32°F), and, of course, frostbite may occur when skin temperatures dip more than a few degrees below 0°C. A skier must take great care that small exposed areas of the face, the nose, ears, and cheeks in particular, do not become so chilled by the cold wind that they fall below the freezing point.

One hears incredible tales of the Bedouins of the Sahara desert withstanding sustained heat and lack of water, and also of the cold-tolerance of Yaghan Indians of Tierra del Fuego, who lived in the slush and snow of winter by the warmth of fires and without clothing. The Bedouin protects himself from the intense reflected heat and direct sunlight of the desert sands by wrapping himself within several layers of clothing. The naked Indians of Tierra del Fuego and the aborigines of Australia keep warm sleeping between two fires, which they frequently stoke to keep going through the night.

hot climates

I have taken a sauna bath in Finland at a temperature of 110°C (230°F), believing it was close to the upper limit tolerated by the human body. However, a Dr. Blagden, Secretary of the Royal Society in England, reported in 1775 of experiments in a room, heated to 126°C (260°F), into which he went and remained with some friends for 45 min. A steak which he took with him was cooked thoroughly, but a dog, whose feet were protected from burning, got along perfectly well. A pot of water, which was covered by oil to prevent evaporation, was heated to boiling, while a pot of water with an exposed surface, which could evaporate, stayed cooler. As in all saunas, a man could not remain in the room if the air became humid at these very high temperatures, for he would be scalded. A sauna bath is a small room, with board walls, floor, and ceiling, heated by a furnace, on which there is a container of hot rocks. The wall temperature of the sauna is usually the same as the air temperature, and the air is very dry. If water is thrown on the rocks, it vaporizes, and the air becomes humid. A person in the sauna would feel an immediate intensification of the heat.

Let us use the conditions in the sauna bath to describe how our bodies react to very hot temperatures. When one enters a sauna the air is stifling at a temperature of 110°C (230°F), but he finds that he can go on breathing. The only question then is: How long can one survive in the sauna? Immediately perspiration begins to roll off of the body, which has become completely wet because the thermal regulation of the body has activated the sweat glands to expel heat. One becomes warmer and warmer, and, as the capillaries dilate from the heat, the skin becomes redder and redder.

A boundary layer of air adheres to all surfaces because of the viscous property of air. In the sauna this layer of air remains next to the skin, and across the layer of air there is an abrupt temperature gradient from the skin temperature of 40–45°C (104–113°F) to the air temperature of 110°C (230°F), as well as a humidity gradient from the saturated air next to the skin surface to the very dry air of the room. This boundary of air is a protection, acting as an insulating cushion around the body. The boundary layer of air, which adheres to all of us, is shown in the Schlieren photograph in Fig. 10.

figure 10. *Schlieren photograph of the profile of a child's face showing the insulating boundary layer of air at the surface.*

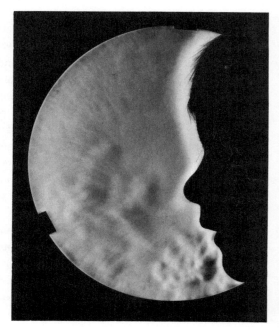

At the time that I was in a Finnish sauna, I wondered what would happen were I to destroy the insulating layer of air separating my skin from the searing heat. By blowing on the back of my hand, I blew away the boundary layer of air and caused the hot air of the sauna to come into contact with my skin. The hot air burned my skin, leaving a red blister. I also felt a slight burning sensation at the tips of my nostrils where breathing had permitted some of the hot air of the room to contact my nose.

So we see that man can take intense heat for limited periods of time because of his ability to perspire and wet the skin and because of his heat capacity, the capacity of his body mass to absorb a certain amount of heat before his deep body temperature will begin to rise. When the air and wall temperature of the sauna is much greater than the skin and body temperatures, the heat can flow in one direction only, i.e., from the hot air to the body. If one remained in the room indefinitely, then the body temperature would eventually creep up to the room temperature, and death would result.

What about the hot deserts of the world? How does man manage to exist in them? How does the nomad or shepherd of the desert tolerate the heat load subjected to his person? The answer is fairly simple. He perspires. Man turns on his evaporative cooling system when on the desert, just as he does in the sauna. But he also takes precautionary measures and stays out of the midday sun where, according to Noel Coward, one would find only mad dogs and Englishmen. The Arabian Bedouins wear a loose-fitting, long white burnoose of wool. This garment permits evaporative cooling by perspiration at the skin surface. Often in the hottest weather they will wear several layers of loose-fitting clothing. A European man, dressed in tropical helmet, lightweight short pants, and a short-sleeved khaki shirt, finds himself miserable during the heat of the desert summer.

The climate of the desert during the summer day is one of very hot air, up to 50°C (122°F) or more, very hot sand, whose surface temperature is 60° or 70°C (140° or 158°F), brilliant direct sunlight, strong reflected sunlight, and very dry air. A hot desert tends to be windy because the large amount of heat at the surface produces much heating of the air near the ground, and this creates buoyancy, which causes instability and much air movement. Deserts are typically windy places. Hot winds blowing across the surface of a person warm him by convective heat transfer. While air which is cooler than the skin or clothing surface will take heat from it by convection, air which is hotter than the surface will deliver heat to it and, thereby, add to the heat load imposed on man during a hot desert day. The radiation intensity of the open desert is enormous and delivers an incident flux of as much as 2.0 cal cm^{-2} min^{-1} of radiation on each square centimeter of the clothing or skin surface. Of this incident flux about 1.4 cal cm^{-2} min^{-1} is absorbed by the clothing surface. Although a person or other object whose surface temperature is 40° or 45°C (104° or 113°F) will emit energy by radiation to the extent of about 0.8 cal cm^{-2} min^{-1}, it is evident that an additional 0.6 cal cm^{-2} min^{-1} must be dumped through evaporative cooling, since convection will add heat or at best have relatively little influence. When a gram of water is evaporated, 580 cal of energy are consumed. The surface area of a man is taken as approximately 1.7 m^2. Let us consider how much water a man must lose by means of evaporative cooling if he absorbs a net amount of heat of 0.6 cal cm^{-2} min^{-1}. The metabolic heat generated inside the body is normally about 0.3 cal cm^{-2} min^{-1}. Hence, the total energy to be dissipated is 0.9 cal cm^{-2} min^{-1}. The surface area of a nude man is 1700 cm^2. If he is in the sun 12 h a day, or 720 min, then the number of liters of water which are evaporated from his surface must be 0.9 cal cm^{-2} min^{-1} × 1700 cm^2 × 720 min × ($\frac{1}{580}$ g (grams) cal^{-1}) × ($\frac{1}{1000}$ g liter^{-1}) = 19.0 liters of water. This is approximately 1.6 liters of water lost per hour. The highest rate of water loss measured for men working intensively for short periods of time is 4.2 liters per hour, and men have had perspiration rates of 3.0 liters per hour for 4-h intervals giving a total loss of 12 liters of fluid. This is an impressive figure when one considers that the total amount of water in the blood is about 4 liters. However, the water lost in perspiration comes primarily from the body tissues. If the net heat load is 0.6 cal

cm^{-2} min^{-1}, it is possible that a man could dissipate this heat by sweating for a 12-h period. However, if the net heat load was substantially greater than this, he would be in deep trouble.

A man losing a lot of water while subject to intense heat becomes extremely thirsty, but, paradoxically, he does not drink enough to replenish the loss even when given an adequate water supply. Tests have shown it to be difficult for an individual to drink much more than one liter in one minute, and when this is done there is very little desire to drink more. An average man weighs about 80 kg (kilograms) or 80,000 g (grams). If he loses 19.0 liters of water in a day this is 19,000 g of water or 23.7% of his total body weight. Tests have shown that if 2% of his body weight is lost by perspiring, thirst becomes violent; at 4% loss of body weight the mouth and throat feel dry, and one feels apathetic, sleepy, impatient, and manifests a lagging pace. At 6% these symptoms increase, and at 8% one can no longer salivate, the tongue feels swollen and sticky, and speech becomes difficult. This is what old desert prospectors referred to as "cottonmouth." Beyond about 10% loss of body weight by perspiring we do not really know the symptoms well, except that the lethal limit for man is when he loses about 18-20% of his body weight in this way. We do know that at a water loss beyond 10% man can no longer care for himself, and beyond 12% he can no longer swallow, and must have forced water in order to recover. There are accounts of men going several days on the desert without water. An extreme case from which recovery was made was that of a man who wandered near the Mexican border for eight days with only one day's water supply.

A man undergoing dehydration caused by perspiring under hot conditions has a rise of body temperature. At a dehydration of 10% the temperature rise is $2°C$ ($35.6°F$) for the resting man, but a $2°C$ temperature rise results in 6-7% dehydration in a man who is exercising or performing work. At some point there is an explosive rise of body temperature, and death ensues when the deep body temperature in man exceeds $41-42°C$ ($106-107.8°F$).

table 8

	rate of perspiration evaporation $(g\ h^{-1})$		
condition	35°C	40°C	45°C
Marching, nude, sun	935	1165	1375
Marching, clothed, sun	640	910	1120
Marching, clothed, shade	490	730	960
Sitting, nude, sun	385	615	800
Sitting clothed, sun	280	460	610
Sitting, nude, shade	220	360	475
Sitting, clothed, shade	245	305	375

The 19,000 g of water loss in 12 h is approximately
1580 g per hour. Tests were made on subjects at Yuma, Arizona, during summer days. Table 8 gives some interesting com-
parisons. One can notice that a rate of water loss of 1580 g per
hour is high, but he should realize that substantially higher
rates may be encountered. The main problem for man is sustaining such a rate for several hours. In fact, it is evident that
man would not survive this rate of perspiration for 12 h and
would need to find shade or perish.

metabolic rates

Metabolic rates for men vary, depending upon the amount of
activity, between about 60 and 400 kcal h^{-1} (kilocalories per
hour) or 0.06 and 0.4 cal cm^{-2} min^{-1}. Stated in another way,
metabolic rates represent food consumption per man of between 1440 kcal day^{-1} and 9600 kcal day^{-1}. Usually
food intake amounts to the equivalent of about 2700–
3600 kcal day^{-1} when man is sedentary or very active,
respectively. It is obvious that the highest metabolic rate mentioned above, i.e., 400 kcal h^{-1} or 9600 kcal day^{-1}, can be
maintained only for very short periods of time. Military per-
sonnel in the Arctic are found to require about 3900 kcal
day^{-1}. Metabolic rates for human beings in various activities
are given in Table 9, where they are expressed in various units
for convenience.

From inspection of Table 9 one can evaluate the relative
role of metabolic rate in humans, in comparison with other
heat sources within the environment. We are all familiar with a

table 9

condition	cal cm^{-2}min^{-1}	kcal h^{-1}	W	Btu h^{-1}
Basal metabolism, age 50	0.058	59.5	69	236
Basal metabolism, age 20	0.067	68	79	270
Basal metabolism, age 5	0.100	102	120	410
Normal active rate	0.219	227	263	900
Men active on the moon	0.247	252	293	1000
Brisk game of tennis	0.370	378	440	1500

75-W light bulb. The amount of heat it generates is approximately the same as the amount of heat an older person generates while resting. However, a child 5 years of age has a basal metabolism of 120 W. This is the age when basal metabolism is at a maximum. It is no wonder a child stays so warm when asleep and does not require many blankets. Many people cover a child with too many blankets, and the child struggles to get out from under them. A normal, active adult generates metabolic heat equivalent to 263 W or 0.219 cal cm^{-2} min^{-1} which is more total heat than is given off by most light bulbs and is less than the radiant heat coming from surfaces of our surroundings. The metabolic rate nearly doubles when one is playing a brisk game of tennis. A man while walking on the moon generates 293 W of metabolic heat, or the equivalent of 0.247 cal cm^{-2} min^{-1} or 1000 Btu (British thermal units) h^{-1}. By comparison, a surface at 25°C (77°F) radiates 0.6 cal cm^{-2} min^{-1}. Normally the amount of metabolic heat generated is small compared with the amount of heat delivered to the body from the environment, but if the environment is very cold, then the metabolic body heat is a more significant proportion.

cold climates

Man in a very cold climate may endure frostbite, snowblindness, skin damage, or undue loss of body heat, resulting in hypothermic injury within the body. Immersion in water at temperatures of −2° to 1.7°C (28° to 35°F) may result in death in 7-15 min. Prolonged exposure to cold results in vasoconstriction of the blood vessels, which drastically reduces the flow of blood in the skin and extremities and ultimately results in tissue anoxia. Prolonged exposure to cold may result in constriction of blood flow to the skin and extremities. When skin temperatures drop to 10°C (50°F) the skin becomes insensitive to pain. Once deep body temperature drops below 35°C (95°F) thermal control is lost, and drowsiness and coma ensue. Death results when body temperature falls below about 26°C (78.8°F). Frostbite, which is the most frequently encountered injury from cold, involves the actual disruption of cellular tissue through the formation of ice crystals, some dehydration of protoplasm, loss of blood circulation, and oxygen starvation of tissue.

The Yaghan Indians of Tierra del Fuego and the aborigines of Australia are famous for their ability to withstand cold. Sometimes stories concerning such peoples become exaggerated. They may not actually undergo the extremes of cold attributed to them in such stories, and in fact they do protect themselves against extreme cold. It is known that these people sleep between two fires at night. Certainly the night is the coldest period of the day, and if these primitive peoples can survive the night, when sleep is necessary, they will survive the day. Physiologists have studied these people and tried to emulate their habits in order to ascertain just how adaptation has occurred. These tribes are now disappearing and are now wearing clothing. Physiologists' observations of these people were made during the 1950s before it was too late to make such studies. They were afraid that the Pitjandjara, the desert tribe of Australian aborigines, would lose their adaptation to cold by wearing clothing and that we might never learn about the unique physiological adaptation of these people.

The custom of the Pitjandjara natives spending the night in the central Australian desert was to build a windbreak of eucalyptus and acacia branches. To the leeward of this they built two fires between which men would lie, either singly or two men back to back. They usually had to stoke the fire between three and ten times during the night, but otherwise they lay quietly, sometimes snoring. The physiologists making the study carried out the same procedure. They lay naked between two fires and found that they had to stoke them from eleven to fourteen times during the night and that they did not sleep well during the intervals. They experienced a weird sensation of simultaneous perspiration and goose pimples as the fires heated one side of the body and the cold sky chilled the other parts. On windless, cold nights, it was possible to sleep a little, but on windy nights conditions were nearly unbearable. Skin temperatures, deep body temperatures, and metabolic rates of the sleepers were measured. The skin temperatures were usually lower in the natives than in the scientists, but they all dropped to between $12°$ and $15°C$ ($53.6°$ and $59°F$) on the cold parts and went up to $45°C$ ($113°F$) on the side facing the fire when the air temperature went down to $0°C$ ($32°F$). These skin temperatures, which were frequent experiences for the natives, were painful to the scientists. By contrast, when the scientists spent these cold nights in their lightweight sleeping bags their skin temperatures remained above $33°C$ ($91.4°$) even at their feet. When no fires were used, and both natives and scientists spent the night nude in lightweight sleeping bags, the metabolic rates of the scientists fluctuated a great deal, while those of the natives remained nearly constant. The scientists were restless and shivering much of the night, and the natives lay motionless all night shivering only a little when they arose in the morning. The feet would cool down to $15-17°C$ ($59-62.6°F$). This was distressingly cold for the scientists, but it did not disturb the natives in the least. When the skin temperatures of non-cold-adapted Europeans drop to $19°C$ ($67.2°F$), shivering usually begins. It became clear from these studies that the Australian aborigines have a much greater tolerance to chilling than European men, but in order to sleep through cold nights the natives do modify their physical environment by building fires and windbreaks.

There were early reports from explorers in North America of Indians being poorly clothed and suffering considerably from the cold. They shivered at night and a great deal while sleeping. On the other hand, Eskimos and Lapps have warm clothing and do not subject themselves to greater cold stress than we do. An interesting experiment was done in Norway in the mountains. Eight men volunteered to live and hike above tree limit for six weeks during September and October wearing light summer clothing. The air temperature at night fell to between 5° and 0°C, and the men spent the night naked inside a single-blanket sleeping bag covered with a thin wind cover. At first the men were miserable, sleeping little at night, shivering much of the time, and thrashing about constantly. After about a week they were able to sleep through the night and remain warm from head to foot. The metabolic heat generated by these eight men increased as the result of their shivering, a movement which eventually became compatible with sleep and rest.

Man in the arctic or antarctic must protect himself against the intense cold and strong winds. The punishment to which explorers in Antarctica are subjected is illustrated by the following report written by Norwegian scientists during a traverse in Dronning Maud Land in the summer 1951 to 1952.

At noon today the warmest temperature measured was $-33°$C $(-27.4°$F$)$. We really feel that it is late in the season, the days are growing shorter, the sun is low and gives no warmth, katabatic air currents blow continuously from the south with gales and drifting snow. When we made camp this evening it was $-37°$C $(-34.6°$F$)$. The inner walls of the tent are like glazed parchment with several millimeters thick ice-armour, at places even one centimeter thick. Every night several centimeters of hoarfrost accumulate on the walls, and each time you inadvertently touch the tent cloth a shower of ice crystals falls down in your face and melts. The sleeping bags are wet and never get time to dry before they freeze. In the night large patches of hoarfrost from my breath spread around the opening of my sleeping bag and melt in the morning.

The whole front of my sleeping bag is like a well starched dress shirt, and last night when I had to pass urine (cold diuresis) the zipper was frozen fast and I spent some time in thawing it loose. The shoulder part of the sleeping bag facing

the tent-side is permeated with hoarfrost and ice, and crackles
when I roll up the bag. The reindeer fur mattress is soaked
through and stands out in a half circle after freezing in a
rolled up state. The ski boots never dry and freeze as soon as
you go out in the morning. When camp is broken and you try
to put on your skis you find the soles frozen in the wrong
angle on your feet. The stiff leather chafes our feet and
Valter has acquired tendovaginites. When the boots are taken
off the insides are quite covered with white frost several millimeters thick and our woolen socks are usually frozen fast and
have to be torn loose, the rime is scraped out with a spoon.
For several weeks now my fingers have been permanently
tender with numb fingertips and blistering at the nails after
repeated frostbites. Valter has his nose and right cheek frost-
bitten.—All food is frozen to ice, ham, butter, tins, etc., and it
takes ages to thaw out everything before being able to eat. At
the depot we could not cut the ham, but had to chop it in
pieces with a spade and threw ourselves hungrily at the chunks
and chewed with the ice crackling between our teeth. You
have to be careful with what you put in your mouth. The
other day I put a piece of chocolate from an outer pocket
directly in my mouth and promptly got a frostbite with
blistering of the palate.

Date 16/9 1950, minimum temperature $-38°C$ $(-36.4°F)$
maximum $-32°C$ $(-25.6°F)$, wind speed 9 m/sec (wind chill
index 2200–2000). Peter and I started homeward at noon in
radiant sunshine but with a bitterly cold wind. The first hour
was a nightmare, trying to hold the dogs on the trail, to protect one's face from the wind, to keep the sunglasses free from
snow and hoarfrost, to thaw out cheeks and nose, where white
frostbite spots reappeared with few minutes interval, sometimes in one place, sometimes in another, to get your mittens
back on your ice cold, stiff fingers between each thawing-out,
the whole time keeping pace with the sledge on your skis.
Your one hand had to juggle with the tow-rope to the sledge,
with the ski-pole, with your mittens, trying not to drop them
and to keep them from blowing away, while thawing out a
frostbite with your bare other hand, the sunglasses milky and

frosted again, your fingers stiffening and aching. Always twisting your head and your parka hood in a vain attempt to shield the face from the tormenting wind and at the same time peer forward along the trail against the wind—well, then you damn the whole Antarctic!*

On the other hand, if the air is still, and the sun is shining in Antarctica, the warmth from incident radiation upon the human body can be very great. In fact, the warmth of the sun can be equivalent to raising the air temperature as much as $25°C$ ($45°F$) if there is no wind. This is equivalent to raising an ambient air temperature of $-5°C$ ($23°F$) to $+20°C$ ($68°F$), which makes it possible for men to work outdoors stripped to the waist in subzero air temperatures. According to the Norwegian scientists quoted above, the radiation was so intense, during the sledging in Dronning Maud Land at the height of summer, that traveling was done mostly at night in order to spare the dogs from the heat load. Even though there was a midnight sun, the sun was low in the sky at night, and the incident radiation at night was less than in the daytime. The rate of heat absorption by the double-walled pyramid tents was so great that, during the daytime, one could lie practically naked on top of the sleeping bag with the tent entrance wide open, while the air temperatures were well below freezing. Even when the sky is overcast, the intensity of the scattered and reflected radiation is so great that life in a tent can be very warm indeed.

The distinctive properties of the Antarctic climate are not only the fierce winds and incredible cold, $-88.3°C$ ($-127°F$) being the coldest ever recorded on earth at the Vostok station, but also the intense amount of radiation. During the sunlit period of the year, the extremely clear air and its low water vapor content allow almost full strength of the direct sunlight to reach the white snow surface on the ground, from which the light is reflected to any other objects on the surface. When the sky is overcast, there is not the usual reduction of light

*Ove Wilson, Norsk Polarinstitutt, Skrifter Nr. 128 (1963), pp. 1–32.

which is encountered in the temperate and tropical regions of the world. This is because the cloud-light penetrating the cloud base is reflected several times between the snow cover on the ground and the clouds overhead. In other regions of the world the amount of light on cloudy days may be reduced to 25% of its value on clear days. In Antarctica the reduction may be to only 50% of the clear day value. Antarctica is very windy because of large cyclonic vortices which form over the southern oceans and move from west to east across Antarctica. Local drainage winds are very common on this continent when the very cold dense air, formed over the high interior plateau, flows toward the sea down the glaciers and slopes. Winds of 20–25 mph are frequent and much greater winds are common. These down-slope winds are known as *katabatic winds* and can be highly variable and fierce, causing intense blizzards and much drifting snow. New snowfall is not particularly heavy in many parts of Antarctica, since the frequent blizzards are primarily a rearrangement by the winds of the snow which already covers the surface.

Scientists interested in the survival of men in cold climates have defined a *wind chill factor* based on the cooling power of the wind. The following formula, which is purely empirical and without a good theoretical justification, is, nevertheless, useful for describing the relative cooling power of the wind. It was worked out about 1940 by Paul Siple from experiments conducted at Little America in Antarctica. Dr. Siple was the eagle scout who accompanied Richard E. Byrd on his first Antarctic Expedition in 1928. The reader may skip the formula and understand the text without any difficulty. If H = the wind chill or rate of heat loss in kilocalories per square centimeter per minute, V = the wind speed in meters per second, and T_a = the air temperature in degrees centigrade, then:

$$H = (\sqrt{100\,V} + 10.45 - V)\,(33 - T_a) \tag{1}$$

This formula assumes that the wind chill represents heat loss from skin at 33°C (91.4°F). The wind chill factors encountered range from 50, which is considered hot, to 2500,

table 10

wind chill factors and stages of relative human comfort

wind chill factor (kcal m^{-2} h^{-1})	*stages of relative human comfort*
600	Very cool. Considered comfortable when dressed in wool underwear, socks, mitts, ski boots, headband, and thin cotton windbreaker while skiing over level ground at 5 km h^{-1} with metabolic heat output of 200 kcal m^{-2} h^{-1}.
800	Cold
1000	Very cold. Unpleasant for skiing on overcast days.
1200	Bitterly cold. Unpleasant for skiing on sunny days.
1400	Freezing of exposed human flesh depending upon amount of radiation, circulation, etc. Skiing or living in a tent becomes disagreeable.
2000	Skiing or living in tent becomes dangerous. Exposed flesh will freeze in 1 min.
2300	Exposed flesh will freeze in less than $\frac{1}{2}$ min.

Source: Ove Wilson, Norsk Polarinstitutt, Skrifter Nr. 128 (1963), p. 9.

considered to be intolerably cold. Some values and their interpretation are given in Table 10.

Experiments in Antarctica have shown that all cases of frostbite occurred at wind chill factors between 1400 and 2100. At Maudheim in Antarctica, which is on the coast, the wind chill factor was over 1400 on more than half the days of the year. With a wind speed of 22 mph (10 m sec^{-1}) exposure at a temperature of $-8°$C (18°F) for 1 h or $-30°$C ($-22°$F) for 1 min will cause human flesh to freeze.

Rather than thinking in terms of the wind chill factor itself, it is more convenient for people to think in terms of an equivalent temperature which represents the temperature still air would need to have in order to give the same wind chill factor as the actual air temperature with wind of a certain speed. In Table 11 the equivalent temperatures are shown. For example, if the air temperature is actually $-6.7°$C (20°F), and the wind speed is 5 mph, the equivalent temperature is $-8.9°$C (16°F). But if the wind speed is 25 mph, then the equivalent tempera-

table 11
wind chill table[a]

mph	dry-bulb temperature (°F)																
	35	30	25	20	15	10	5	0	-5	-10	-15	-20	-25	-30	-35	-40	-45
	equivalent temperature[b] of wind chill index (°F)																
calm	35	30	25	20	15	10	5	0	-5	-10	-15	-20	-25	-30	-35	-40	-45
5	33	27	21	16	12	7	1	-6	-11	-15	-20	-26	-31	-35	-41	-47	-54
10	21	16	9	2	-2	-9	-15	-22	-27	-31	-38	-45	-52	-58	-64	-70	-77
15	16	11	1	-6	-11	-18	-25	-33	-40	-45	-51	-60	-65	-70	-78	-85	-90
20	12	3	-4	-9	-17	-24	-32	-40	-46	-52	-60	-68	-76	-81	-88	-96	-103
25	7	0	-7	-15	-22	-29	-37	-45	-52	-58	-67	-75	-83	-89	-96	-104	-112
30	5	-2	-11	-18	-26	-33	-41	-49	-56	-63	-70	-78	-87	-94	-101	-109	-117
35	3	-4	-13	-20	-27	-35	-43	-52	-60	-67	-72	-83	-90	-98	-105	-113	-123
40	1	-4	-15	-22	-29	-36	-45	-54	-62	-69	-76	-87	-94	-101	-107	-116	-128
45	1	-6	-17	-24	-31	-38	-46	-54	-63	-70	-78	-87	-94	-101	-108	-118	-128
50	0	-7	-17	-24	-31	-38	-47	-56	-63	-70	-79	-88	-96	-103	-110	-120	-128

very cold

bitterly cold

extreme cold

[a]Wind speeds greater than 40 mph have little additional chilling effect.
[b]Equivalent in cooling power or exposed flesh under calm condition.

Source: Mimeographed report, ESSA, Washington, D.C.

ture is −26.1°C (−15°F). If the actual air temperature is −17.8°C (0°F) and the wind speed is 5 mph, the equivalent temperature is −21.1°C (−6°F). If the wind speed is 40 mph, the equivalent temperature is −47.8°C (−54°F). It is customary for the weather reports from many U.S. stations to give the equivalent temperature during winter days, in addition to giving the actual air temperature and wind speed. One should dress according to the equivalent temperature during severe cold conditions, rather than according to the actual air temperature. A skier can make an approximate assessment of the equivalent temperature if he can estimate approximately how rapidly he is moving and if he knows the actual air temperature. Table 11, the wind chill table, is not completely consistent with Dr. Siple's wind chill factor formula. Some liberty was taken with adjusting values for very light winds and low air temperatures. Nevertheless, it is the table used by the U.S. weather services for weather reports.

In very cold climates one frequently finds people wearing more clothing than they need while exercising and wearing less than they need while resting. In order to maintain thermal equilibrium in any given environment, the optimum insulation required is five to six times as much when one is at rest as at work. The primary purpose in the design of arctic clothing is to provide body insulation by means of dead air spaces in small pockets and at the same time to allow for the ventilation of perspiration. Polar explorers have cautioned against the danger of sweating profusely and forcing moisture into the outer layers of clothing, where it freezes and greatly increases the conductivity of the clothing. Condensed moisture on the outer layers causes increased accumulation of perspiration inside the clothing, and this exaggerates further the loss of insulation against the cold.

human comfort

Having just considered extreme climate conditions, both hot and cold, and their effects on man, we should consider briefly the matter of comfort. The human being is quite tolerant to the particular conditions of heat or of cold when they become

uncomfortable. Because of individual variation to comfort
conditions, it is necessary to express the percentage of the
population which finds a particular set of conditions as comfortable or uncomfortable.

Shown in Fig. 11 are the comfort zones, expressed in terms
of the relative humidity and the air temperature for normally
clothed persons, sitting still indoors without any substantial
amount of air movement. The regions marked "cool,"
"warm," and "hot" are the results of purely subjective response to outdoor circumstances with normal amounts of
wind and sunshine. It is certainly true that in conditions of
humidity and air temperature to the left of the left-hand
0% lines all persons will feel cool, and to the right of the
right-hand 0% lines all persons will feel hot. It is interesting to
note that most people acclimatize to summer temperatures
which are about 5°C (9°F) warmer than the winter temperatures they find comfortable. These data were collected in the
days prior to substantial amounts of household and office air

figure 11. *Percentage of people in the United States
comfortable indoors in the winter (solid line) and in the
summer (dashed line) as a function of relative humidity
and air temperature.*

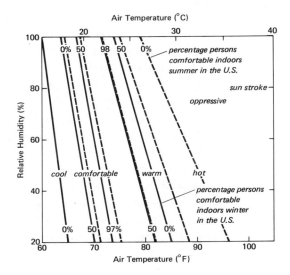

conditioning. I am certain that a somewhat different result would be achieved now with many Americans accustomed to summertime air conditioning. We do know that some people tend to keep their homes cooler in summer than they do during the winter. Most people are likely to desire an outdoor summertime temperature slightly higher than the wintertime temperature indoors.

The reader should note how the comfort lines in Fig. 11 slope toward lower air temperature for higher relative humidity. In humid air at a certain temperature one is as comfortable as in very dry air which is approximately $5°C$ ($9°F$) warmer. During winter months one can have a comfortable home at a lower temperature with some saving of fuel if it is well humidified. Outdoor air at a temperature of $0°C$ ($32°F$) and a relative humidity of 80%, when it is heated to $22°C$ ($71°F$), will have a relative humidity of 18%. According to the comfort chart, about 50% of the people would be comfortable inside. In order to make this air comfortable for 97% of the people, the air would need to have moisture added to it to bring it to a relative humidity of about 55%.

People living in different countries acclimate to very different comfort zones depending upon their general habits. Many people in England are quite comfortable during winter months at an indoor air temperature of $15°C$ ($60°F$), whereas, according to Fig. 11, no one in the United States would consider himself comfortable at this temperature. The indoor comfort for the people of Batavia, Java, shifts upward in air temperature about $3-4°C$ ($5-6°F$) compared with the comfort zone for Americans during the winter.

During the summer of 1959 the U.S. Weather Bureau (now the National Weather Service) began publishing a Discomfort Index, which was later called the THI (Temperature-Humidity Index), and this is still in use today. Values of THI are calculated with one of the following linear equations, depending upon the type of input data available. The dry-bulb air temperature, T_d, must be known. Whether T_w, the wet-bulb temperature, T_{dp}, the dew point temperature, or rh, the relative humidity, is known determines the equation used for the calculation of THI.

$$THI = 0.4 \, (T_d + T_w) + 15 \tag{2}$$

$$THI = 0.55 \, T_d + 0.2 \, T_{dp} + 17.5 \tag{3}$$

$$THI = T_d - (0.55 - 0.55 \, \text{rh}) \, (T_d - 58) \tag{4}$$

The THI is plotted in Fig. 12 as a function of the air temperature and relative humidity.

When the THI reaches 70, ten percent of the population is uncomfortable, at 75 half the population is uncomfortable, and at 80 just about everyone is uncomfortable. Comparison of the new THI with the older comfort chart reveals some disagreement. The new index suggests that people are generally comfortable at a warmer temperature for a given relative humidity.

human health

Climate affects the health of man in several direct ways and in many subtle indirect ways as well. Climate begins to influence

figure 12. *The THI and the percentage of people uncomfortable as a function of the relative humidity and the air temperature.*

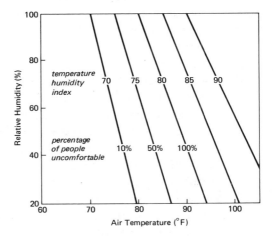

our well-being from the time of conception, throughout life until death. It is generally believed that babies conceived during the very hot months of the year lack the vitality of those conceived during the cold months. The state of the health of a mother during pregnancy affects the well-being of the fetus and the health of the baby at birth. There also seems to be some evidence that the fetus is affected by the air pollution a mother breathes and that the health of the newborn carries these effects with it throughout life. Weather and climate affect our health directly by inducing conditions, such as sunstroke, heat exhaustion, snow blindness, and frostbite. Indirect effects of weather and climate are changes in metabolism, body chills or wetness, or other symptoms which reduce the body's resistance to disease. Climatic conditions may also be responsible for exhaustion or reduced mental and psychological vigor. Increased nervousness and high blood pressure are sometimes associated with passing storm systems, while depression, irritability, and lethargy are attributed to the passage of warm fronts. There seem to be increased automobile accidents with falling pressure, although it is self-evident that storms will directly increase the accident rate.

One suspects that a climate with constant weather conditions would not be advantageous to man and that a certain amount of variability is desirable. Changing conditions act as physiological and psychological stimuli. The tropics represent those parts of the world with the least seasonal thermal variation. The people living there have a greater incidence of disease and seem to have less vitality and vigor than those living in other climates. A lack of vitality can occur in many populations from a lack of protein in the diet, a situation which is common in the tropics. Ellsworth Huntington, a Yale University geographer, has suggested in his theory of climatic determinism that civilization has emerged most strongly in those parts of the world with the most stimulating climates. Before man wore much clothing, he may have been constrained to live in warmer climates where the environmental temperature was about $30^{\circ}C$ ($86^{\circ}F$) but, as he learned to protect himself with clothing, he could adapt to life in more invigorating climates.

It would appear that the optimum temperature for physical comfort is definitely greater than the optimum temperature for mental vigor, so the theory of climatic determinism would indicate more rapid evolution of thought and inventiveness as man moved into the temperate regions of the world. Students will be interested to learn that Huntington detected a seasonal variation in the performance of mathematics students at the West Point Academy which correlated with climate.

The rise and fall of the Greek and Roman civilizations certainly raises many questions concerning climatic determinism. The spectacular ascent of the Greek culture between 500 B.C. and 300 B.C. is very striking, yet one knows that more than simply a favorable climate was necessary for this to occur. One wonders why it is that in modern times the Greek nation is unable to recover the intellectual and inventive vigor of the past and become a leader among modern nations. What has held back these fine people? Was it climate and agriculture or climate and disease? Certainly the Greek valleys with their undrained marshes were prolific breeding grounds for mosquitoes and, thereby, for the transmission of malaria. In fact, all Mediterranean lowlands were susceptible to such infection, but the lands of Greece were among the worst areas of malarial infection in Europe. Many scientists agree that the general debilitation of the Greek people was related to the high incidence of malaria.

After the defeat of the Carthaginians at Zama in 202 B.C. the Romans extended their empire into the eastern Mediterranean. The Roman Republic existed from 509–527 B.C., and the Roman Empire, which succeeded it, went into serious decline toward the end of the first century A.D. Yet the populations of Rome, Alexandria, and Constantinople continued to grow, and Rome itself may have exceeded 2 million people by the end of the fifth century A.D. The Pontine Marshes surrounding Rome were famous breeding grounds for diseases such as malaria and plague. Once again, was it this infection of a large part of the population which led to the debilitation of the Roman Empire? Or was it the fact that agricultural production declined because of depleted soils combined with a changing climate of hot dry summers, which prevented grazing of animals for lack of summer pasture? It was no doubt a combination of all things climatic, sociological, and political which brought the downfall of the Roman Empire and the invasions by Goths, Huns, and Vandals. Gibbon described it this way in his famous work entitled *Decline and Fall of the Roman Empire:*

The winds might diffuse that subtle venom, but unless the atmosphere be previously disposed for its reception, the plague would soon expire in the cold and temperate climates of the earth. Such was the universal corruption of the air that the pestilence which burst forth in the fifteenth year of Justinian was not checked or alleviated by any difference of the seasons. In time its first malignity was abated and dispersed; the disease alternatively languished and revived; but it was not till the end of a calamitous period of 52 years that mankind recovered their health or the air resumed its pure and salubrious quality. The triple scourge of war, pestilence and famine affected the subjects of Justinian and his reign is disgraced by a visible decrease of the human species, which has never been repaired in some of the fairest countries of the globe.

Were the invaders a stronger more energetic people because of the cooler climates from which they came and because of a high protein meat and milk diet? Rome was sacked by Goths in A.D. 410 and A.D. 455. Huntington showed that the Caspian Sea had a minimum level at about A.D. 500, and he attributed the collapse of the Roman Empire to deficient rainfall as follows: "At the time of Christ, the return of favorable climatic conditions did much to help Rome recover her prosperity but two centuries later there began a decline in rainfall which was one of the main causes of Rome's collapse." Studies have shown that rainfall and humidity seemed to decline in southern and eastern Europe after the time of Christ until about A.D. 1200, and this may have upset the delicate pastures of the Asiatic steppes and resulted in the later invasions of Europe by the Mongolian hordes. Whether this is actually what did happen and whether climate had a significant influence on these peoples is difficult to know for certain. It does raise a number of interesting questions concerning climates and civilizations.

Malaria is a parasitic disease which induces chills and fever in man. In severe cases it results in brain damage and anemia from which death may occur. The malaria infection is caused by a parasite of the genus *Plasmodium* which is transmitted by the genus of mosquito known as *Anopheles*. There are at least 60 different species of *Anopheles* which transmit the malaria parasite. When a mosquito bites a person and sucks in malarious blood, the parasites mate and produce cysts which form on the stomach wall of the mosquito. When the cysts are ripe, they burst open and their spores, called sporozoites, move to the salivary glands. When the mosquito bites a person these sporozoites are injected into the blood stream; they are transmitted to the liver where they produce large numbers of parasites. The parasites release metabolic products in the liver which are carried by the blood stream throughout the body. These metabolic products upset the temperature regulating system causing chills, fever, and sweating. The necessary resident time within the mosquito is from one to three weeks, and the rate of development depends upon the mosquito's temperature. Now we can see that climate affects the incidence of malaria in several ways. From rainfall pools of standing water are created where the mosquitoes can breed. They will not breed in running water. Temperature affects the rate of development of the cyst and the frequency with which the parasite is transmitted from the mosquito vector to the man as a host. If there is much standing water, but very cold temperatures, as in northern regions of Canada, Siberia, etc., then malaria is not a problem, for the parasite will not develop. If there is standing water and warm temperatures, the incidence of malaria can be great, and large numbers of people are affected. If people are few and far between, then the rate of infection is much less than where large populations of people exist. The flying radius of the mosquito vector may be as short as a quarter mile.

Many malarial mosquitoes live in houses, as well as in marshes and damp forests, thereby bringing the vector distance down to a few feet. Hence, it is easy to understand why large concentrations of people in Egypt, Greece, and Italy were particularly vulnerable, since they lived in areas of warm climates with rainfall and standing water. Malaria existed in North America as far north as the St. Lawrence River, in Europe from England and the northern Dvina River, and to Lake Baikal in Asia. Through the use of DDT, drainage of swamps and wet places, and the systematic spraying of kerosene on standing water, malaria has been virtually eliminated from most parts of the world, except in Africa and Asia where perhaps 150 million cases of malaria still exist today.

There is always a segment of any population which complains of ill health or a lack of well-being during the course of certain weather events. During the passage of frontal systems many types of complaints and purported illnesses apparently occur. However, it has been impossible to prove cause and effect in such instances.

The passage of a warm front is marked by falling barometric pressure, rising air temperature and humidity, upslope air, stratus clouds, and upslope rain. Many people complain of irritability, of feeling depressed, of malarial attacks, and of the occurrence of perforated ulcers at times of passage of warm fronts. The passage of a cold front is associated with rising barometric pressure, falling air temperature and humidity, large scale turbulence in the atmosphere, and the formation of cumulus clouds. People often seem to experience stimulation, exhilaration, and general well-being during the passage of cold fronts, but some people complain of pleurisy and similar ill effects.

Rapid changes of weather conditions, such as the alteration of warm and cold fronts, may appear to be depressing or stimulating, as well as to induce cardiovascular disease and result in an increase in fatalities. The most famous phenomenon of purported weather-induced health effects seems to be that of the foehn wind of the Alps, and of the Chinook wind in the Rocky Mountains. The foehn and Chinook winds are great rushes of subsiding air across mountain ranges. On the leeward side of the mountains the air rushing downslope suddenly becomes very warm because of a rapid increase in pressure. The air is moving rapidly, and the result of a sudden pressure increase is an explosive, adiabatic, warming of the air, often by as much as 15-20°C (27-36°F). The physical symptoms attributed to foehn winds are such subjective phenomena as headache, nausea, sleeplessness, lethargy, irritability, a general feeling of debility, and more objective phenomena, such as increased pulse rates and a drop in blood pressure. In fact the purported health response to the foehn or Chinook winds is very similar to that which is believed to come with the passage of warm fronts.

The author can speak personally of often experiencing the Chinook winds while living in Boulder, Colorado. The temperature, just prior to the arrival of the Chinook, may be about -5°C (23°F), and within a couple of hours it will rise to 10°C (50°F). Whatever snow may have covered the ground melts rapidly because of the high temperature and strong winds. The winds are extremely gusty and turbulent, sometimes reaching speeds of 70 mph or more. I found the Chinook winds extremely disturbing. If the Chinook arrived at night, as it often seemed to do, I would sleep fitfully, seemingly awake most of the night, and fully conscious of debris blowing against the house and of tree branches swaying against the roof. The feeling of irritability the next day must have resulted from insufficient sleep the night before, although, I must admit, I rarely, if ever, had a headache and never the feeling of nausea. I actually dreaded the arrival of a Chinook wind, for I knew in advance that it meant loss of sleep for me, a feeling of fatigue and a lack of initiative or ambition. As far as I could ascertain the sleeplessness for me was entirely a matter of the noise generated by the wind in whistling through the cracks of the window frames and the blowing about of objects against the house. It did not seem to me that my response was the direct result of the rapid change in atmospheric pressure. Also I was adjusted to sleeping on these cold winter nights in a cool bedroom, and with the onset of the Chinook the room was no longer as cool. In any case, the temperature influence was certainly secondary to the noise effect.

Some who have studied the human health effects of foehn or Chinook winds are convinced that the pressure changes are directly responsible, but others who have looked into the matter as objectively as possible are convinced that there is no clear-cut evidence showing any unique effect upon the human body. Certainly, however, there seems little doubt that the indirect effect of foehn or Chinook winds is a real phenomenon. Likewise the induced responses to the passage of warm or cold fronts of some people are real and are the result of many simultaneous changes in environmental conditions, including temperature, humidity, radiation from variation of cloud cover, wind, and noise level.

sunburn or tan

One aspect of climate, which can be either pleasant or painful to people, is the effect of ultraviolet radiation from the sun in the form of tan or sunburn. Until recent years, man's health has been dependent upon exposure to sunshine, but because of the use of vitamin D in foods today man is able to avoid rickets, which at one time resulted from vitamin D deficiency, caused by insufficient exposure to the sun. In fact, the necessity for sunlight to penetrate to the deeper layers of the skin where the photochemical formation of vitamin D occurs appears to be the reason that people in northern latitudes, where the amount of sunlight is minimal during the long winter months, are light-skinned. Also it is known that too much vitamin D produces serious toxic effects in the body, which may explain the evolution of dark-skinned people in sunny climates, where transparent skin and constant exposure to the sun would have given them too much vitamin D.

Sunburn is caused by a narrow band of light in the ultraviolet between 2800 Å (angstroms) and 3200 Å. However, solar radiation shorter than 2900 Å is absorbed in the atmosphere by ozone and does not reach the earth's surface. A layer of ozone, formed in the stratosphere at a height of about twenty miles above the surface, effectively screens the ground from the most actinic of the sun's rays and protects organisms, including man, from serious ultraviolet burns. On the other hand, tanning of the skin is produced by a broad band of sunlight of wavelengths between 3000 Å and 4100 Å, and the chemical events are completely different than in the case of sunburn. Hence, if people with light, transparent skins have a thin protective layer of ultraviolet absorbing pigment, such as suntan oil, spread over the exposed skin surface, then tanning can occur without sunburn. Getting a tan is fashionable among light-skinned people, and the production of suntan oils is a big business today. Millions of dollars are spent annually by vacationers seeking the sunnier climates of the world where they can relax in the sun and tan themselves. While skiing or climbing in the high mountains, one is exposed to substantially more ultraviolet radiation than one receives near sea level, where the additional dust and moisture content of the atmosphere weakens the ultraviolet.

Light-skinned people seem to get more skin cancers as the result of frequent exposure to the ultraviolet rays of the sun. Farmers, as a group, have a greater incidence of skin cancer than the population as a whole does.

5
animals
and
plants

We have learned in earlier chapters about the weather and the climates of various regions of the world. We have studied the significant factors, such as radiation, temperature, wind, and moisture, which are used to describe climates. We have classified climates according to the vegetation types occurring throughout the world and also according to human comfort. We have discussed regional climates and microclimates. The behavior of man in various extreme climates was described, as well as man's accidental and intentional modification of climates. We have discussed the physiology of man as it affects his response and adaptation to various climates. Now it is important that we understand the responses of plants and animals to climate and weather. This is a very large subject, of which we can give only a limited number of examples. Perhaps it was easier to understand the effects on man first and then to look at the rest of the living world upon which we depend so inexorably. We must understand what it is about the climate that affects any organism. Why should sunshine, rain, wind, heat, or cold affect a plant or an animal?

All life on earth depends upon the primary productivity of the green chlorophyll-laden plants of the world. How is a plant coupled to the climate? What are the mechanisms which govern the living system in response to the climate factors we have described? The ecosystem earth is a very complex system of animate and inanimate components. Mankind can no longer afford to exploit the biotic and abiotic resources of the world. We are now faced with a critical challenge to understand the dynamics of ecosystems if we are to live in harmony with the communities of plants and animals upon which we depend. An important part of the detailed web of understanding ecosystems is to know the response of animals and of plants to climate.

animals

Animals of every kind, insects, reptiles, amphibians, mammals, birds, etc., respond to climate in many different ways. Climate is always present throughout the life history of an organism. Temperature, whether it be the temperature of the air, of the water, of the soil, or of the walls of a burrow, is truly a ubiquitous factor, and for terrestrial animals in the open air thermal radiation is ubiquitous also. Humidity is known to be a significant factor in the behavior of most animals, and wind is also important in determining animal behavior. The temperature of an animal is the result of energy flow between itself and the environment. Metabolic heat is generated within all animals, and nearly all animals lose energy by evaporative cooling, which is the result of moisture loss by breathing. An animal also exchanges heat by radiation, by convection, and by conduction. It can make physiological adjustments to keep from getting too hot or too cold, but it can also move about in the environment in order to select a proper combination of radiation, air temperature, air movement, and humidity for energy balance. Each and every species of animal behaves in a unique way to the climate nearby. This behavior is a response to the exchange of energy.

Cold-blooded animals, the *poikilotherms*, can tolerate body temperatures from below or near freezing to about 45°C (113°F) or more. Warm-blooded animals, the *homeotherms*, have more specific body temperature requirements, and they can tolerate relatively little variation in body temperature, except during hibernation. The warm-blooded animal regulates its body temperature by means of temperature sensors located in the midbrain near the hypothalamus. These sensors generate appropriate physiological responses of metabolism, such as perspiration, panting, blood flow, and control other factors, including body posture, location, and activity. By contrast, the cold-blooded animal has relatively little control of his body temperature by means of physiological adjustments, and he must achieve comfort by moving into the proper environment or through the appropriate orientation of his body. Microscopic organisms, such as bacteria, protozoa, plankton, and spores will always have temperatures equal to the temperature of the medium in which they are immersed. Insects will usually have temperatures within a few degrees of the air temperature, but when they are exposed to sunlight, some of the larger insects are substantially warmer than the air. It is also true that when they are in shade, some insects are cooler than the air because of evaporative cooling.

Animals migrate in response to the seasonal variation of climate. Some animals hibernate when environmental conditions become cold, some animals become dormant in winter, and others simply change their manner of living throughout the season. Mammals may grow a thicker coat of fur as winter approaches, or put on more body fat. Insects often develop a resistance to freezing by increasing the glycine content of their protoplasm and reducing the water content and concentrations of salts and body fats. It is interesting to note that many insects are substantially more resistant to cold as winter approaches than they are in the late spring as summer comes on. Although there is enormous variation in the low temperature tolerance of insects, many can withstand temperatures down to −20°C (−4°F), some even lower, yet many cannot withstand temperatures below about −5°C (23°F). In the same way, there is a considerable variation in the tolerance of insects to heat. Fifty degrees centigrade (122°F) seems to be the generally accepted maximum temperature limit for most insects. Early work suggested that fleas could not withstand temperatures higher than about 32°C (89.6°F), which must make the flea one of the least heat tolerant of all insects. The tsetse fly, which transmits sleeping sickness to cattle, cannot withstand high temperatures and therefore lies in wait among the green leaves of the forest until the cattle come nearby. Then it darts out, alighting on the animal, feeding, and infecting. It then returns to the cool shadows of the forest. The sunlit backs of the cattle, or even their shaded sides, are often too warm for the tsetse fly to remain there long and survive.

Lizards cannot survive body temperatures of less than about 2° or 3°C (35.6° or 37.4°F), nor above about 48°C (118.4°F), while snakes are limited to a temperature range of −3°C (26.5°F) to 43° or 44°C (109.4° or 111.2°F).

Although there is a minimum temperature above which an animal will survive and a maximum temperature below which it will survive, the animal does not function well until some intermediate temperature exists. The intermediate temperature, at which the animal is most active or at which it achieves maximum development in minimum time, is known as the optimum temperature. The optimum temperature range may be very narrow, or it may be very broad. Generally the temperature response relation for an organism will have a shape similar to the curve shown in Fig. 13. If the temperature is above or below the optimum temperature, the rate of development or of activity is retarded. Now it is easy to understand why it is that an insect population, a field of plants, or a population of animals will suddenly burst forth in great abundance. If the climate conditions are just right for a particular insect, then it can grow quickly and perhaps produce many generations in a period of a few weeks. This may be exactly what happened to the diamondback moth when it underwent a population explosion, followed by a mass exodus. The situation is described later in this chapter. The codling moth, which does serious damage to apples and was accidently introduced into North America from Europe, has an optimum temperature which is

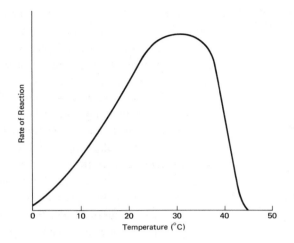

figure 13. *Relative rate of reaction of biochemical events as a function of temperature.*

fairly warm. In New England the warmest part of the summer is of sufficient length for the codling moth to have only one generation a year, but in the Shenandoah Valley of Virginia it has two or more broods, and in the Ozarks it may have three broods in a single summer season, causing great destruction to the apple crop.

insects

The seasonal variation in the abundance of insect pests is strongly related to climatic conditions. It is not simply the general climate, i.e., the average weather taken over a long period of time (30 years), which is necessarily meaningful to an insect, but the variable weather conditions which exist moment by moment. Not only must the adult survive a sufficient length of time to hatch a new generation, but each stage of insect development, e.g., the egg, pupa, larva, or various instars, must have suitable conditions for survival and growth to maturity. Each stage may have very different temperature or moisture requirements.

Rain may constitute an advantage or a disadvantage to an insect population. Rain may supply the moisture to grow the plant, which the insect feeds on, it may wash the eggs from the leaves where they have been deposited by the female, or it may flood and drown the pupae in the soil where they are hatching. Rain, of course, supplies water for puddles where mosquito eggs and larvae can grow abundantly. The Japanese beetle, which was so disastrous to crops in the United States after its introduction here in 1916, spends its egg and larval stages in the roots of ornamental plants. There must be adequate moisture during June, July, and August, or there will be heavy mortality of eggs and larvae. In the United States, spring, summer, and autumn rains affect the abundance of the Hessian fly, whose population increases with increased rains.

Studies of the pale western cutworm show that the main factor influencing its abundance is the amount of rainfall in spring and summer of the year preceding an outbreak. The critical amount of precipitation in the period May to August is 4–5 in. When precipitation is above 5 in., there is a decrease in the cutworm population the following year, but when the precipitation is under this, there is an increase.

Temperature always has a significant effect on insect populations. The critical temperature below which larvae of the Mediterranean fly remain inactive is $14°C$ ($57.2°F$), and for larvae of the Hawaiian fly it is $16°C$ ($60.8°F$). It is known that the rice stem borer in Japan appears with maximum intensity when the July temperature is between $24°$ and $26°C$ ($75.2°$ and $78.9°F$), while at the same time there is rainfall between 150 mm and 250 mm. We are all familiar with the increased chirping of crickets when the weather gets warm. The higher the temperature, the greater the number of chirps per minute. If the thermometer reads between $7°C$ ($45°F$) and $27°C$ ($80°F$) and you add 37 to the number of chirps you count in 15 sec, you get the correct air temperature in degrees Fahrenheit.

The pine shoot moth is a pest which inflicts severe damage to red pines and Scotch pines in the United States and Canada and has recently become a threat to the great ponderosa pine stands of the western United States. Study showed that the pine shoot moth had a distribution which appeared to be restricted along its northern boundary by very low winter temperature. Investigations confirmed this and revealed the reasons for the moth's survival in the regions where extensive damage does occur. Adults emerge in early summer and lay their eggs on pine shoots. The eggs hatch in about two weeks. The larvae feed on the buds of pine shoots until August, when they bore into the buds and stay there for the winter. If the pine shoot is covered by snow, then the bud and its guest stay warm enough to survive most winter cold, and the following summer it can emerge in great numbers to vent its fury on the pine forest once again. However, if the snow does not cover the pine shoots, or if it becomes sufficiently cold above the snow for a long enough period for the cold to penetrate to the shoot and kill the larvae, then it will not survive the winter. Hence, winters of deep snow are precursors of summers of great potential damage to the pine forest by the pine shoot moth.

The boll weevil is the single most limiting factor to cotton production in the United States. A temperature of $-17.8°C$ ($0°F$) is fatal to the boll weevil, but the cotton belt never encounters a temperature this low. A summer of hot, dry weather appears to limit the boll weevil, while during wet summers the weevil does heavy damage to the cotton crop.

Dry weather in the spring encourages the abundance of the chinch bug, and warm moist weather encourages a fungus disease which attacks the chinch bug and keeps it in check. In years when large forested areas are affected by drought so that trees lack vigor, certain bark beetles, such as the southern bark beetle and the hickory bark beetle, become very destructive. They are brought into check once again if very wet weather prevails during a sufficiently long period of time.

Very often the influence of climate on an insect population is indirect and complicated. The green bug does much crop damage over wide areas from Texas to Minnesota, when there is a cool, wet spring. This is because the parasites which attack the green bug are kept in check during cool wet weather and cannot work on the population of green bugs. Relationships are often much more complicated than this one with climate affecting the entire food chain of plants and animals and the predator–prey relationships.

One of the most dramatic of climate factors influencing the distribution of insects is wind. Often great numbers of insects are picked up by the wind and transported hundreds of miles. One of the most striking occurrences of this was the invasion of England and parts of Scandinavia by the diamondback moth during the summer of 1958. This small moth is a pest of cruciferous crops, such as cabbage or radish. Although it is always present in Britain in some numbers, its population there was increased suddenly by a large invasion of moths transported by a strong easterly air stream on 22 June 1958. The population buildup had occurred in eastern Europe near Estonia, Latvia, or Lithuania, or perhaps in the Soviet Union, followed by either an ecological or meteorological stimulus for exodus and was transported by wind over a distance of nearly 2000 miles.

Another interesting case of the wind affecting insect distribution is that of the western caterpillar, whose larvae devastate the coniferous forests of Vancouver Island. When there are westerly winds the greatest population density appears on the eastern side of the peninsula, where, because of the foehn wind effect, there are more sunny days and temperatures are more favorable. On the western side of the island there is much orographic rain (rain caused by air rising up mountain slopes) and clouds making the caterpillar population smaller.

In parts of north Africa and the Middle East great masses of locusts are transported by the wind over considerable distances. When airborne the masses of locusts are so dense as to have the appearance of a large dark cloud which is undulating and changing shape as it moves. Once on the ground again, the voracious and avaricious insects consume all vegetation in their path. It must be a terrifying experience to witness the descent of a cloud of locusts upon one's own garden.

The African locust arrives in the Canary Islands when there is a high-pressure system (anticyclone) bringing southeasterly winds to the islands, or when a depression or low-pressure system brings southeasterly winds. Either situation produces warm relatively dry air in the Canaries. At these times, the locusts are not only brought in, but thrive to devastate crops and vegetation.

mammals

The warm-blooded mammals, whose body temperatures are between $36°$ and $40°C$ ($96.8°$ and $104°F$), adapt to a wide variety of climates. They do so by altering many of their physiological and physical properties. When climate varies from cold to warm, an animal with a constant body temperature must change one or more of its body factors affecting heat exchange if it is to remain in thermodynamic equilibrium. The body properties which affect the heat exchange between the animal and its environment include metabolic rate, evaporative water loss rate, amount of body fat, fur or hair thickness, body surface area, length of appendages, blood flow to the skin surface and appendages, surface coloration, and the body temperature itself. Most mammals die if the deep body temperature falls $15-20°C$ ($27-36°F$) below the normal body temperature or rises $3-6°C$ ($5.4-10.8°F$) above normal. Thus the upper lethal temperature is much more critical than the lower lethal deep body temperature.

Domestic cattle generally thrive in cooler climates. Beef cattle can withstand substantially warmer conditions than dairy cattle. The Brahman cattle are particularly hardy for hot climates, apparently the result of a highly functional skin, which has more sweat glands per unit surface area than in European breeds of cattle. The sweat glands are located closer to the skin surface in the Brahma, which renders them more responsive to heat stress. The Brahma loses about six times more water by perspiration, when conditions are hot, than through respiration, whereas other cattle lose only about three times more by perspiration than by respiration. The large pendulous neck folds of the Brahma apparently play a very small role in the heat regulation of the animal. The metabolic rate of the Brahma is 20% less than that of European cattle. A lower metabolic rate means less internal heat and better ability to withstand a greater external heat load and warmer climates. The European domestic cattle have relatively compact bodies and moderately heavy coats of hair, which aid their adaptation to cool climates. By contrast, most subtropical breeds of cattle have rangy frames, large appendages, and thin coats. The yak, found in eastern and central Asian mountains, has a thick, stubby body with a short neck and short legs. Cattle will normally put on a thick coat of longer hair for the winter and shed this for a thinner coat in the spring and summer. The change in coat quantity is initiated by *photoperiod*, i.e., by the increasing daylight rather than by warmer temperatures. The winter coat of hair has a fine thick pelage among the longer hairs. In tropical regions the length of day is nearly constant throughout the year, and shedding of hair occurs all the time. Horses, ferrets, mink, and other animals also vary their coat thickness with season on a photoperiod mechanism.

Holstein cows, kept at 29°C (84.2°F) for nine weeks, adjusted to this warm environment by reducing metabolic rate and food intake, increasing evaporative water loss, increasing internal conduction by means of blood flow to the skin, and by reducing the density of the coat. If an animal can perspire, it has a distinct advantage for heat adaptation over the animal which can only pant. Most animals' tolerance to heat is determined largely by their ability to perspire profusely. However, an animal can maintain a high rate of perspiration for only a limited period of time. An animal in a warm environment will lose the ability to thermoregulate, above a certain temperature, and its body temperature will rise. This usually occurs when the environmental temperature is between 28° and 32°C (82.4° and 89.6°F). In lactating Holstein, Jersey, Brown Swiss, and Brahman cows the deep body temperature begins to rise at environmental (air) temperatures of 21°C (69.8°F), 24°C (75.2°F), 27°C (80.6°F), and 35°C (95.0°F). If the heat load is not too severe, an animal can achieve thermoregulation with an increased body temperature, but if the thermal stress is too great, then thermoregulation is destroyed, and hyperthermia results. This will occur at a lower air temperature, if the animal is exposed to high humidity and much solar radiation, than it would were the animal exposed to dry air and shade from the sun. On the other hand, when exposed to severe cold, a mammal increases its metabolic rate, reduces blood flow to appendages, has piloerection of its hair, and reduces evaporative water loss. A large animal does not need to produce as much increase in metabolic rate as does a small animal, because of the greater insulation from the larger animal's body fat and fur. Thermal regulation is lost when the environmental temperature drops below a certain level, and then body temperature begins to drop. This state is known as hypothermia, a condition which is reached in the guinea pig at an environmental temperature of $-15°C$ ($5°F$), $-25°C$ ($-13°F$) in the rat, and $-45°C$ ($-49°F$) in the rabbit. Again it is clear that the environmental temperature at which hypothermia will occur depends upon the amount of incident sunlight, the humidity, and the amount of wind.

I saw many dead cattle following an intense blizzard which struck eastern New Mexico and western Texas in late March 1970. The air temperature did not drop below about $-10°C$ ($14°F$), but the wind speed was 30 mph or more so that the wind chill factor was high. The total snowfall was very little, but during the peak of the storm there was complete white-out, and visibility was reduced to zero. The snow piled three or four feet deep around snow fences, ditches, and automobiles. Testimony to the ferocity of the storm were the hundreds of automobiles nearly buried by drifting snow in the ditch or by the side of the road. In places where there is open range, some cattle, blinded by the driving snow, had wandered with the wind until they mired in deep snow, which accumulated along a railroad track. Here they no doubt thrashed about to extricate themselves, which produced an increase in metabolic rate, increased body heat, and increased perspiration. The wind-driven snow penetrated the hair, and the increased body heat melted it, wetting the fur and causing a loss of insulation. The increased body heat could then escape rapidly from the body causing the body temperature to drop. Some cattle were still standing on all fours, frozen dead in their tracks, while many had fallen over.

Sheep exhibit many of the same adaptive features for adjusting to environmental conditions as cattle. Sheep in cool climates have compact bodies, short legs and necks, small ears, and thick, dense coats of wool. The sheep of northern deserts have less compact bodies and wool, longer legs and ears, and distinctive fat tails. The sheep of the southern Sahara and south Indian deserts have slender, long bodies, long legs and necks, long ears and tails, and fine short hair. Sheep use rapid panting as a means to expel moisture and a great deal of heat. Some sheep can increase their rate of panting tenfold from a resting respiratory rate of 20–30 per minute to between 200–300 per minute. Sheep lose relatively little water through perspiration. During a hot desert day sheep show a rise of deep body temperature from $39°$ to $41°C$ ($102.2°$ to $105.8°F$). Desert sheep have a lower metabolic rate than do other races of sheep. Goats are well adapted to desert conditions. Their small slender bodies and thin coats assist heat loss. The goat under heat stress pants at half the rate of the sheep and does not perspire as much, although the sheep does not perspire a great deal either.

Horses have the ability to perspire profusely, and they do so when they are generating a lot of body heat during hard work. The Arabian horse, with its slender body, is well suited to warm climates, while in cold, wet, windy regions, such as Scotland, the Shetland pony is well adapted with its stubby body, short legs, and long, thick hair. The donkey, as well as the zebra, is very heat tolerant with its small body, long legs, large ears, and short-haired coat.

Among animals it is interesting to note the extent to which weather and environment affect the season of birth. Most animals will optimize the chance for survival by giving birth at the most favorable times of the year. The optimum season of birth in north temperate zones is the spring of the year. Porcupines and deer breed in the autumn, since their periods of gestation are four and six months, respectively, while beavers with a three- or four-month period breed in late winter, and cottontail rabbits breed in the spring, since they give birth about twenty-seven days after conception. Among certain marsupials, those animals carrying their young in pouches, the length of time young stay in the pouch is different among species, but, nevertheless, they all leave the pouch at the same favorable season. One exception to this is the red kangaroo, which is a continuous breeder. The red kangaroo lives in a region of prolonged drought and irregular rainfall. In order to ensure survival it is bringing young into the world continuously. When there is good pasture because of rainfall, some of the young survive, but when it is very dry, they may perish.

It is always the small mammals with short gestation periods that are most susceptible to the weather. A most striking behavior is exemplified by the swamp rabbit of southeastern Missouri. During a very wet spring when the habitat for these rabbits was flooded, litter resorption occurred in a large percentage of the population. The same sort of behavior was observed among populations of cottontail rabbits. There are, of course, many unanswered questions in the entire phenomena of animal breeding and environmental stress. Weather is just one factor among many. The weather prevailing throughout the breeding season may have a direct or indirect influence, such as through the amount of available food supply.

energy budget of animals
energy flow

An animal is coupled to the climate surrounding it by energy flow. One realizes that any animal must remain in energy balance most of the time. Animals are often in transient states for limited periods of time, but over a sufficiently long time interval they must be in energy balance. While the warm-blooded animal requires its temperature to be more or less constant, the cold-blooded animal can allow his temperature to vary over a considerable range. The description of the energy balance in physical terms is essentially the same for warm-blooded or cold-blooded animals. How a particular animal achieves energy balance is strikingly different for the warm-blooded and the cold-blooded animals. Hence, it is appropriate to describe first how any animal is coupled to its environment and what factors it has at its command for remaining in energy balance.

The pertinent parameters of the environment which describe the climate near an organism are radiation (solar and thermal), air temperature, wind, and humidity. What do these seemingly dissimilar quantities have in common? What does the organism derive from them? What single factor does the organism need? All life requires energy. Every living process, whether it is cell division, cell enlargement, photosynthesis, metabolism, respiration, blood flow, or breathing, does work and consumes energy. The energy must come from the environment in the form of nutrients, or as light and heat.

We live in a thermodynamic world—in a world of heat and cold. All life exists at a definite energy level. It is only at absolute zero that the level of energy in the world is zero, but above that temperature all events are driven by energy. Although there is a seemingly unlimited amount of energy in the world, the energy level or temperature level at which we live is vital to our survival. We function most efficiently at some optimum temperature and therefore at a particular energy level. Although the primary source of energy on earth is the sun, we derive heat from thermal radiation, exchange energy with the air by convection and by evaporation, and convert chemical energy into proteins and warmth by means of metabolism.

Metabolic heat, M, is generated within the animal from the food he consumes. Additional energy is acquired as an animal absorbs incident radiation, in the form of direct sunlight, scattered skylight, reflected light from clouds and other surfaces, and thermal radiant heat from all nearby objects. The actual amount of radiation absorbed by the animal's surface depends upon his geometry, his exposure, and the absorptivity of his skin, fur, or feathers. The total amount of radiation absorbed by his surface we shall designate R.

The surface of the animal emits infrared thermal radiation according to the fourth power of the absolute temperature T_s of the surface. This is the result of a well-known law in physics. The actual expression for the quantity of radiation emitted per unit area is $\epsilon \sigma T_s^4$, where ϵ is the emissivity of the surface, σ is the Stefan–Boltzmann constant, and T_s is measured in degrees Kelvin. Energy is lost by convection from the surface of an animal to cool air nearby according to $kV^{1/3}\,D^{-2/3}$ $(T_s - T_a)$, where V is the wind speed in centimeters per second, D is the diameter of the animal's body in centimeters, T_a is the air temperature, and k is a constant. The rate of heat lost by convection is proportional to the cube root of the wind speed over the surface, and inversely proportional to the two-thirds root of the diameter. If the air nearby is warmer than the animal, then heat is delivered to the animal by convection. When water is evaporated, energy is consumed. As an animal expels moisture by breathing, water is evaporated into the air from the lungs and energy is expended. Some animals can perspire over their surface and cause further energy loss by evaporative cooling. Not all animals have the ability to perspire. In fact, relatively few animals produce some degree of thermal regulation by perspiration. Man can perspire profusely when the heat load becomes too severe for his body physiology. The amount of evaporative water loss (from respiration and perspiration), expressed in energy per unit area per unit time, is given here by the symbol E. It requires 580 cal per gram of water to evaporate water from liquid to vapor at a temperature of 30°C (86°F). One additional energy exchange mechanism may occur. That is energy exchange by conduction C if the animal is in physical contact with a colder or warmer substrate. If the substrate is colder than the animal, heat is conducted from the animal to the substrate, which would likely be the ground or a rock.

theory

The energy balance for the surface of an animal can be written as follows:

$$M - E + R = \epsilon \sigma T_s^4 + kV^{1/3}\,D^{-2/3}\,(T_s - T_a) + C \tag{1}$$

I wish the story of energy exchange between the animal and the environment were simpler than this, but this energy balance equation describes properly the interaction between the animal and his climate. In what follows we will neglect the conduction term.

A particular animal species of given size and description will have certain values of M, D, and E, as well as of absorptivity to incident radiation (which is included in R). An animal can vary the values of M, D, and E within certain limits. The climate determines at any moment the values of V, T_a, and the quantity of radiation incident on the animal (which is included in R). Hence, all independent variables in Eq. (1) are prescribed, either by the animal or by the climate, and the dependent variable, T_s, the surface temperature of the animal, adjusts to a value such that the energy budget balances. If the amount of incident radiation on the animal increases, then the surface temperature will increase, providing all other quantities remain unchanged. If the air is cooler than the animal, and the wind speed increases, the surface temperature will decrease in order for the energy exchange to balance. If several factors vary simultaneously, the surface temperature may change up or down. If the combination is just right, the surface temperature may remain unchanged.

The rate at which metabolic heat can flow out from the body cavity through the insulating layers of fat, fur, or feathers depends upon the temperature gradient between the deep body temperature T_b and the surface temperature T_s and also upon the quality of insulation by fat I_b and by fur or feathers I_f. The effective or net amount of heat generated within the body cavity is the metabolic heat M less the evaporative water loss E caused by respiration. Hence, the rate of net heat production $(M - E)$ within the body cavity is given by:

$$M - E = \frac{T_b - T_s}{I_b + I_f} = \frac{T_b - T_s}{I} \tag{2}$$

where $I = I_b + I_f$, the total insulation of fat and of fur or feathers. The simultaneous solution of Eqs. (1) and (2) represents the response of the animal to its environment at all times. If we eliminate $M - E$ from the two equations by substitution we get:

$$T_b - T_s = I \ [\epsilon\sigma T_s^4 - R + kV^{1/3} \ D^{-2/3} \ (T_s - T_a)] \tag{3}$$

The next few paragraphs may contain more mathematics than many readers care to follow; however, it is included here for those who will find it useful.

If the body temperature is fixed, as with a homeotherm, then the surface temperature adjusts so that Eq. (3) balances. For a cold-blooded animal, where a constant body temperature is not required, the body temperature will relate to the surface temperature through the insulation mechanism described by Eq. (2). If $M - E$ is very small, as it often is for some reptiles, then T_b and T_s are nearly the same. In any event $T_b - T_s = I(M - E)$. The quantity R is the energy input to the animal by all fluxes of radiation which are absorbed and is a rather complicated function for an animal in the open, particularly during the daytime. However, if the animal is in a blackbody cavity, such as a burrow, room, or cave, for which the air temperature and the wall temperature is the same, then $R = \epsilon\sigma T_a^4$. Hence, the term:

$$\epsilon\sigma T_s^4 - R = \epsilon\sigma \ (T_s^4 - T_a^4) \cong 4\epsilon\sigma \ T_a^3 \ (T_s - T_a) \tag{4}$$

This was obtained mathematically by a Taylor's expansion of the quantity $(T_s^4 - T_a^4)$ and by using the first approximation only, which gives the above linear form. It is, however, an approximation which is accurate only when $T_s - T_a$ is small. The student with sufficient mathematical training can verify this for himself. If the expression given in Eq. (4) is substituted into Eq. (3), one gets the following:

$$T_b - T_s \cong I(4\epsilon\sigma T_a^3 + kV^{1/3}D^{-2/3})(T_s - T_a) \tag{5}$$

Often one finds in books describing the energetics of animals the following oversimplification:

$$M - E = \frac{T_b - T_s}{I} \quad \text{and} \quad M - E = C(T_s - T_a) \tag{6}$$

or

$$T_b - T_s = IC(T_s - T_a) \tag{7}$$

This makes the assumption that C is a constant. Clearly it is not a constant, since $C = 4\epsilon\sigma\, T_a^3 + kV^{1/3}\, D^{-2/3}$. However, in still air or in air of a constant flow rate, V is a constant, and if the air temperature T_a is a constant, then for a given animal of fixed dimension D the quantity C will be constant. The requirements for constancy are many, and generally the assumption that C is constant is not justified, and C is, in fact, a variable.

The energy budget equation for animals applies just as well to man. For some animals and for man it is necessary to partition the energy budget between the appendages (arms and legs) and the trunk of the body itself. The ideas represented in the energy exchange process are the same as before, but the procedure is somewhat more complex.

There is another way of looking at the energy budget equation which differs from the way it is written in Eq. (3), which contains T_s. Usually we know the body temperature of an animal but not the surface temperature. If from Eq. (2) we solve for T_s and substitute into Eq. (1) we obtain the following:

$$\begin{aligned}
M - E + R = {} & \epsilon\sigma\,[T_b - I(M - E)]^4 \\
& + kV^{1/3}\, D^{-2/3}\,[T_b - T_a - I(M - E)]
\end{aligned} \tag{8}$$

Inspection of Eq. (8) shows us precisely how an animal can adjust M, E, and I for a certain set of environmental conditions R, T_a, and V, in order to have a specific, nearly constant, body temperature T_b. This would be the case of a warm-blooded animal. On the other hand, a cold-blooded animal will have relatively little control over M, E, and I but will allow T_b to vary over a large range of values, in response to a certain set of environmental conditions R, T_a, and V. The idea which must be emphasized is the simultaneity of the variables; no single variable, either R, T_a, or V, interacts alone with the animal. They act only together in concert.

climate space

We can now turn the problem around and predict the climate in which an animal must live based on his inherent thermo-dynamic properties. If one knows the following properties of an animal, i.e., metabolism, water loss rate, characteristic dimension, absorptivity and emissivity to radiation, insulation, and body temperature requirements, and, in addition, if one knows the limits or ranges of values for each quantity for which the animal is capable, then one can predict the combination of radiation, air temperature, and wind speed which must exist at any moment for the animal to be in thermodynamic equilibrium. The three-dimensional space of radiation, air temperature, and wind speed we call the *climate space* for an animal. If we include the humidity of the air, then the climate space is a four-dimensional volume.

The climate spaces for the desert iguana and the cardinal are shown in Fig. 14 at a constant wind speed of 100 cm sec^{-1}

figure 14. *Climate space diagram for a cardinal and a desert iguana showing the combined limits of air temperature and of radiation absorbed by the surface of the animal within which the animal must live when the wind speed is 100 cm sec^{-1} (2.2 mph). Increased amounts of absorbed radiation require that the animal is restricted to a lower air temperature. (From* Topics in the Study of Life: The Bio Source Book, *Harper & Row, New York, 1971, p. 394.)*

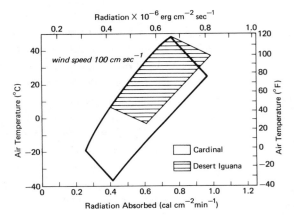

(2.2 mph). The right-hand boundary of the quadrilateral is defined by the amount of radiation absorbed by the surface of the animal in a normal, sunny outdoor environment at midday. When the air temperature is high, there is more radiation available in a given environment than there is when the air temperature is low. Hence, the right-hand boundary slopes from left to right. There are several reasons for this. Normally when air temperatures are higher it is usually summer and midday. When air temperatures are higher the ground surface temperature is higher and the stream of thermal radiation directed upward from the surface is greater. Also when the air is warm there is a greater flux of downward radiation from the atmosphere than there is when the air is cold. In the case of the desert iguana and cardinal climate spaces, the position of the right-hand boundary for the cardinal is further toward the right, or toward greater amounts of absorbed radiation, than for the desert iguana. The reason for this is that the cardinal has a mean absorptivity to direct sunlight of 0.8, while the desert iguana's mean absorptivity is 0.6. The left-hand line of the quadrilateral, delimiting the climate space, is the amount of radiation absorbed by the animal at night, when he is in the open, exposed to the cosmic cold of space and the thermal radiation flux from the ground surface. At night all fluxes of radiation are of far infrared wavelengths, and all animals are essentially "black" to these wavelengths. This means that all animals absorb the same amount of radiation when in the same environment at night. Hence, the left-hand line represents the same boundary for the climate spaces of all animals.

The upper and lower limits of the climate spaces are the true energy limits for the animal when exposed to a given amount of wind. The limiting line approaches the horizontal, i.e., the air temperature, more closely when the animal is small than when it is large and more closely for high wind speed than for low wind speed. This is because the air temperature affects the energy budget of the animal, mainly through the convective exchange of energy. A small characteristic dimension, a high wind speed, or both imply a large coefficient of convective heat transfer and a tight coupling between the en-

124

*man
and his
environment:
climate*

ergy content of the animal and the air temperature. The desert iguana is smaller than the cardinal, and, as a result, has boundary limits which are less steep, more horizontal, and closer to a constant air temperature. The climate space of the desert iguana is distinctly more limited than it is for the cardinal. However, the iguana can remain in full sunshine at a temperature up to nearly 37.8°C (100°F), while the cardinal must seek some shade when the temperature exceeds about 23.9°C (75°F) and the air movement is only 100 cm sec^{-1}.

The ability of the cardinal to withstand low temperatures far exceeded 46°C (115°F), and the birds, in order to survive, sustain temperatures as low as -37°C (-35°F) in wind of 100 cm sec^{-1} when exposed to full sunshine, but the desert iguana would not live if subjected to air colder than -4°C (25°F) under the same circumstances. If there is a strong wind present, calculations indicate the cardinal will not survive an air temperature less than -15°C (5°F), and the iguana will not survive less than 1.7°C (35°F). Each animal would seek a sheltered position. Most animals will not allow themselves to approach their absolute limits for survival too closely. An animal must remain active and alert, particularly when he is exposed to predators, and will be careful not to become too hot or too cold. Most of the time the animal will move within his habitat in such a way that his actual position within his allowable climate space is well within the upper and lower air temperature limits. It is interesting to note that both the desert iguana and the cardinal can sustain an air temperature of nearly 46°C (115°F), when they are shaded from the sun and exposed to the clear cold sky. If the air temperature approaches this temperature or exceeds this value, it is certain that the desert iguana would burrow in the soil where temperatures at a depth of a few inches would be substantially lower, especially where the soil is shaded. The mortality rate among the cardinals would increase significantly if the air temperature exceeded 46°C (115°F), and the birds, in order to survive, would try desperately to find pockets of cooler air while remaining exposed to a cold sky and shaded from the sun.

Another comparison of climate spaces is given in Fig. 15 for

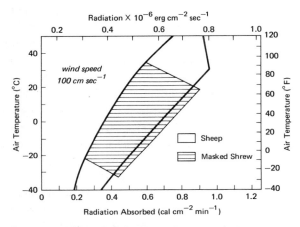

figure 15. *Climate space diagram for a domestic sheep and a masked shrew showing the combined limits of air temperature and of radiation absorbed by the surface of the animal within which the animal must live when the wind speed is 100 cm sec^{-1} (2.2 mph). Increased amounts of absorbed radiation require that the animal is restricted to a lower air temperature.*

the domestic sheep and the masked shrew. The sheep has an incredible range of climate adaptation, while the shrew is much more limited, particularly at high temperatures. The sheep can withstand nearly all air temperatures normally encountered on the earth. The masked shrew cannot remain in sunshine at temperatures greater than 21°C (70°F) at a wind speed of 100 cm sec^{-1}. The shrew lives on the forest floor where the air movement is very low, but the shady leaf litter provides a cool habitat where he can remain on warm days. The masked shrew will not be in exposed habitats or in southern parts of the United States, where summer temperatures at the soil surface, even in the shade, exceed his climate limit. The masked shrew has an unusually high metabolic rate for his body size, and, with the fur insulation he wears, he is able to withstand rather low temperatures, –30°C (–22°F), for an animal so small. The reader should note the very steep upper boundary for the sheep contrasted with the nearly horizontal limit of the climate space for the shrew. The relatively large body size of the sheep essentially decouples his body temperature and energy budget from the air temperature, while the shrew, of small body diameter, has a large convection coefficient and its body temperature is more strongly coupled to the air temperature. However, the sheep will often be in a much windier environment than the shrew, and this will enhance his ability to withstand higher air temperatures when exposed to full sunshine. Once again, however, we should remind ourselves that an animal is not likely to crowd his climate limit too closely, except for limited periods of time when he is forced to do so by circumstance.

The fourth dimension in the climate space, i.e., humidity, has not been worked out for these animals, but this must be done in order to understand their full response to climate. Nevertheless, from the examples presented here the reader can appreciate the necessity to consider the simultaneous influence of radiation, air temperature, and wind on animal body temperature, energy budget, and comfort.

desert animals

Camels are unusual animals and are well adapted to hot, dry desert environments. The camel has a long, lanky frame with long legs and feet, which are well insulated against the heat of the desert sand. The camel can take in enormous quantities of water at a single time. In fact they can increase their body weight by 30% at a single drinking episode. The camel's exceptional tolerance to heat and dryness for long periods of time does not, surprisingly enough, depend upon water storage. The deep body temperature of the camel fluctuates considerably and may rise as much as $6°C$ ($42.8°F$) during a hot day. Since the camel is a large animal, it has considerable heat capacity. With a temperature rise a camel weighing 500 g is capable of absorbing 2500 kcal of heat if its average specific heat is 0.8. This is a great quantity of heat, which the camel then loses by radiation and convection at night while its body temperature cools back down. Camels perspire very effectively but not more than necessary. Camels can go for a week, or longer, without drinking water and have been known to endure a lack of water for seventeen days without serious consequences. A camel will lose up to 27% or more of its body weight by dehydration and not be in serious trouble. If a dog loses more than 12% of its body weight in water, it is likely to die. The surface, particularly the back of the camel, is well insulated with fur. The fur absorbs the sunlight at its surface and is effective insulation above the skin. The fur on the back of a camel exposed to the full summer sun will rise to $80°C$ ($176°F$), while the underlying skin will remain at about $40°C$ ($104°F$). Perspiration takes place at the skin and does not wet the fur in the process.

The jackrabbit inhabits arid and semiarid regions of the United States and often lives where no free water is available. The water it derives must come from the green food it eats. The rabbit apparently has no sweat glands and can lose evaporative water primarily through respiration. However, the rabbit does lose cutaneous water, which produces some evaporative cooling of the skin. When the air temperature is about $40°C$ ($104°F$) or higher the deep body temperature of the rabbit is about $42°C$ ($107.6°F$), and the conductive and convective loss of heat is very small. It is surmised that the large ears of the jackrabbit act as effective radiators of heat. Infrared thermography is an electronic system which makes a picture of the radiation emitted by a surface. Infrared thermography of a rabbit shows that the ears are distinctly hotter than the head and body. It is thought that during the warmest days the jackrabbit may survive the radiant heat of the desert by sitting in a depression, which is screened by vegetation and ground from the reflected sunlight, direct sunlight, and thermal radiation of the hot desert soil. The rabbit's ears can radiate heat to the cool sink of the clear blue north sky whose radiant temperature is about $10°$ or $15°C$ ($50°$ or $59°F$). Daytime air temperatures of $45°C$ ($113°F$) or higher are sustained by a jackrabbit in this manner. Putting together just the right combination of radiation exchange seems to be the only way a nonburrowing, medium-sized animal can survive when it does not have available any substantial amounts of water to use for evaporative cooling. The jackrabbit apparently does not have too much trouble surviving the cold of winter. Calculations show that at night it can take air temperatures as low as $-15°C$ (5.0°F) if there is no wind, or $-12°C$ (10.4°F) in a wind of 2.2 mph. If the air temperatures are much lower, the jackrabbit will not be in the open but in a burrow or protected position where he gains warmth from the ground.

Pack rats and also kangaroo rats inhabit the desert. Whereas the pack rat needs much water under hot conditions and cannot live on dried food, the kangaroo rat can supply all of its water needs from dried food. The pack rat must eat green food, while the kangaroo rat derives metabolic water from the digestion of the food it eats. The normal deep body temperature of the kangaroo rat is 36°C (96.8°F) to 38°C (100.4°F). When air temperatures exceed 30°C(86.0°F) some fatalities occur, and in all cases death ensues if air temperatures exceed about 43°C (109.4°F). Maximum deep body temperature is 41°C (105.8°F). When the heat stress is heavy on the desert, the kangaroo rat can salivate for limited periods of time until it can return to its burrow where conditions are distinctly cooler than they are in the open.

Lizards, snakes, and tortoises inhabit desert regions and many other climate zones as well. These cold-blooded animals are most active when their body temperatures are from 30°C (86.0°F) to 40°C (104.0°F), but they can survive body temperatures as low as 3°C (37.4°F) and as high as 43°C (109.4°F) or 44°C (111.2°F). It has been reported that some desert lizards can survive body temperatures as high as 48°C (118.4°F). Reptiles have relatively low metabolic rates and generally low water-loss rates. However, when they are warmed by the sun their metabolic rates can increase substantially. This will also increase their loss of evaporative water through the skin. Normally the body temperature of a reptile is within a few degrees of the environmental temperature, but in full sun a reptile may get considerably warmer. Lizards scurry across the hot sands of the desert and seldom remain exposed to the sun when the air is hot during midday. At night and during the winter lizards burrow into the soil, where they remain above freezing, and, although they become cool and lethargic, they do not perish from the cold.

A climate space diagram for the giant reptiles shows that they could not withstand moderate to high air temperatures when exposed to the sun. This may have been one of the reasons for the extinction of the giant reptiles. There may have been several forces acting simultaneously which drove these large animals into extinction, but the severe limitation produced by climate could have been an effective factor. If the climate became dry and sunny, and the animals could not remain in the shade of trees or could not find pools of water in which to take refuge, then they would have encountered too much sunlight and air temperatures which were too high.

birds

Birds are truly ubiquitous over the earth's surface, an observation which suggests their enormous adaptability to environment. Birds are warm-blooded animals, whose deep body temperatures are between 40°C (104.0°F) and 42°C (107.6°F). Lethal body temperatures occur at 45°C (113.0°F) to 47°C (116.6°F) and at 36°C (96.8°F) to 38°C (100.4°F). Feathers of birds provide excellent insulation and as a result of high metabolic rates birds can withstand extremely low external temperatures. When conditions are hot, birds depend on the evaporation of water to prevent body temperatures from rising to a lethal level. However, birds do not perspire. The water loss occurs mainly as respiratory loss which birds exaggerate by rapid breathing or by gular fluttering when conditions are hot. Most birds will not be about and active during the heat of the day, particularly during summer months. A bird molts and thins out its feather coat during the warmer season of the year and puts on a thicker coat with more fine down during the cooler season. When a bird is very warm it lifts its wings and exposes the underwind body surface, which has a little feather covering, in order to dump heat by radiation. When it is very cold a bird fluffs its feathers in order to improve the quality of insulation, tucks one leg under its body to reduce heat loss from the extremity, and reduces its breathing rate, perhaps tucking its bill under a wing in order to lower the respiratory loss of water.

agriculture

Climate affects agriculture production in so many ways that it is difficult to select a point from which to begin. The primary factors of climate affecting agriculture are moisture, heat, and light. It is these factors and the exchange of carbon dioxide, oxygen, and nutrients which affect photosynthesis, growth, seed germination, fruit set, and plant productivity. Other factors affecting plant productivity, which are themselves directly influenced by climate, are insects, fungal disease, viruses, and the quality of the soil, a direct result of the weathering of rocks.

Natural plant communities have evolved slowly over a long period of time, during which climate, soil, plants, and animals have interacted in a dynamic manner to form the particular landscape characteristics of regions. It is very difficult to consider the action of one of these general factors without considering the others. For instance, one cannot speak of the influence of soil of plants without also considering the climate and the animals of the same region. One cannot discuss accurately the formation of soil types without including the influence of climate, plants, and other organisms, as well as the availability of certain parent materials, such as the regional minerals that go into soil content. The sun warms the soil and evaporates water from it. The wind removes moisture and warmth from the soil if the air is cool and dry, and it removes moisture from the soil and gives up heat to it if the air is warm and dry. Plant productivity depends on the moisture and heat available in the soil. But the amount of wind near the soil surface depends upon the density of grasses, shrubs, or trees. More wind reaches the soil surface of the prairie than that of the forest. Thus, climate, soil, animals, and plants are inexorably linked together to give us the natural ecosystems.

monoculture versus diversity

Man cuts the forest or plows the prairie to put in its place a *monoculture* of corn or wheat. Man replaces the natural eco-

system and its diversity and stability with a simple plant community. For example, wheat fields which may cover large areas
of land have an inherent simplicity and instability. Because of
this instability, as well as an inability for self-propagation and
self-maintenance, man must manage and cultivate the unnatural system of the wheat fields, or that system will destroy
itself. Left unattended, the fields of grain will quickly degenerate, and weeds of various kinds will begin the slow process of
taking over and creating a more diverse, more stable, and
ultimately natural plant community once again. Man must give
the grain fields an adequate water supply by means of irrigation. He must protect the grain against insect pests, fungal
diseases, weed infestation, and predators, and he must, when
possible, modify the microclimate of his fields through mulch-
ing and windbreaks.

A corn field or wheat field is far more vulnerable to severe
storm damage or to devastation by flood, drought, heat, or
cold than are the native plant communities. We are reminded
of the dramatic impact of the great drought of the mid-1930s
on the wheat fields and native prairies of western Kansas, western Oklahoma, and eastern Colorado. Most of the prairies had
been plowed and put into wheat only to dry up, die off, and
blow away creating the infamous "dust bowl." There were a
few places where the native prairies of buffalo grass, grama
grass, and other species remained unplowed. Although they
suffered from the drought, thinned out to some degree, and
became sparse, they did, nevertheless, retain the sod and survive the extensive drought years as a viable plant community.
Men of the western prairies during the depression years of the
mid-1930s did not have the skills, nor the resources, to manage
the wheatlands through the severe drought in order to avert
the "dust bowl" disaster. Man must, of course, grow wheat for
food, but, in doing so, he must appreciate the vulnerability of
the system he creates. Today our know-how of wheat field
management is sufficiently improved so that it can keep a
wheat field growing through some very dry years, and avoid a
total disaster even though yield will be low. Today the improved management comes from the use of hardier varieties of

wheat, from better plant nutrition through the application of fertilizers, and from a more extensive use of irrigation and shelter belts.

The extensive use of shelter belts in the West was begun during the "dust bowl" period. Although they did not accomplish all that was expected of them, they have proven extremely effective in many ways. A shelter belt is a long barrier of trees, half a mile to a mile or more in length and four or five rows deep, which forms an effective windbreak. The trees planted are combinations of juniper, Russian olive, ponderosa pine, and other hardy varieties, which when they are mature may produce a barrier 30 ft high. Today one sees many of these shelter belt plantings along the roadsides across the western plains. In the beginning some people thought that the shelter belts would take water from deep down in the soil and release it to the air, in sufficient amounts to humidify the air downwind, thereby producing a more moist environment for the wheat fields beyond the shelter belts. This process was totally ineffective, and the amount of humidity change was inconsequential. But the shelter belts did shield the fields from the wind, to a considerable extent downwind and to some extent upwind. This caused great snow accumulation on the downwind side and added considerable moisture to the wind-protected fields. The total effect of the shelter belts was to reduce the wind and increase the moisture on the fields of the western plains. New Zealanders have planted row after row of Monterey pines on the wind-swept Canterbury Plains of their country to break the winds and make life more tolerable for the crops. If man is willing to manage the unnatural ecosystems which he creates for food production, he can succeed to some degree, despite the relative vulnerability of the system to climate and disease. However, despite various levels of success, man must appreciate the extent to which his artificial system is vulnerable and the impending likelihood of disaster at any time.

grains, cotton, and tobacco

Corn, a cultivated plant which originated as a tropical grass, is widely distributed throughout the world between the latitudes

58°N and 40°S. Corn is grown below sea level on the Caspian Plain and above 12,000 ft in the Peruvian Andes. The adaptability of corn to various climates is truly amazing. Strains of corn have been developed to meet great differences of heat, cold, moisture, growing season, light levels, etc. Each climate has its own varieties of corn which do best. Basically corn is a warm-weather crop, which requires both warm days and warm nights. Iowa is one of our best corn-growing regions. It has been said, "It is so warm in Iowa in July that you can hear the corn grow at night." Indeed the corn does continue to grow at night, even though photosynthesis is only in progress during the daytime. Corn will not germinate below 12.8°C (55°F). The region of greatest corn production in the United States has a mean summer temperature between 21° and 26.7°C (70° and 80°F) and a mean nighttime temperature exceeding 14.4°C (58°F). The greatest productivity is achieved by corn when its temperature is between 35° and 37.8°C (95° and 100°F), a plant temperature which is often achieved in midday during the hot summer months, when the plants are in full sunshine and the air temperature is above 32.2°C (90°F). Although corn grows best in warm weather, extremely high air temperatures are injurious when moisture is in short supply and transpiration cannot occur. During the summer of 1966 temperatures near St. Louis, Missouri, exceeded 41°C (105°F) for five days or more. Corn plants showed serious damage by denaturation and desiccation, while the species of the native oak-hickory forest and the native grass exhibited relatively little damage. This is another example of the plasticity and stability of native plant communities, compared with the susceptibility of introduced species, particularly agricultural crops.

Corn requires a good moisture supply throughout much of its growing season. Areas in the United States which have rains between 3 in. and 6 in. per month during June, July, and August have the largest corn yields. A corn plant uses from 260 to 450 lb of water in transpiration for each pound of dry matter produced. Some varieties of corn require relatively little water for good productivity. This is particularly true of certain varieties of corn grown by the Hopi, Zuni, and Navajo Indians of Arizona and New Mexico, as well as those grown by the Mexicans.

Climate affects the insect pests and diseases of corn in a specific way. During 1970 a new variety of corn was planted throughout most of the United States. It was particularly convenient for the hybrid-corn seed growers because the male parts of the plant are sterile. This characteristic prevents self-pollination and means that the seed growers do not need to hire hundreds of people to go through their fields detasseling corn in order to produce good hybrid seed. Because of this convenience most of the corn growers of the country began to use this wonderful new hybrid with the result that a highly vulnerable monoculture existed across the land. In July a fungus, the Southern corn leaf blight, unexpectedly mutated into a form able to infect this particular variety of corn. When a few fields in the South became infected, climate conditions across the country were such that the fungus spread with incredible speed.

The rapid spread of the fungus resulted from persistent southerly winds which swept northward from the Gulf Coast picking up fungal spores in Florida and Georgia and transporting them into the central Midwest. The strong northerly flow of Gulf air continued week after week because of the huge Bermuda high-pressure system off the east coast of the country and the clockwise flow of air around this blocking high pressure. The warm, humid summer air was conducive to rapid fungus growth with the result that the corn crop was quickly infected and severely damaged. America came precariously close to a devastating corn-crop disaster. Average crop losses were about 13%, while losses on some Southern farms were nearly 100%.

There are far more pests and diseases of corn in tropical regions than there are in temperate zones. It is also interesting to note that the flint varieties of corn are much less susceptible to insects than are the dent varieties because of their hard kernel.

Sorghum, which is used extensively to feed cattle, is grown

in many areas which are too hot and dry to grow corn effectively. Sorghum grows best where the mean July temperature exceeds 23.9°C (75°F). If the mean July temperature is 26.7° to 29.4°C (80° to 85°F), sorghum does very well indeed.

Cotton grows best when the mean annual air temperature is above 15.6°C (60°F), where there is a frost-free season of at least 180-200 days, a minimum rainfall of 20 in. per year with suitable seasonal distribution, and a maximum rainfall of 60-75 in. per year. The average summer temperature for the best cotton production should be 25°C (77°F) to 29.4°C (85°F). Considerable sunshine is required for good cotton production. Generally a sunshine condition of more than half the days is required for good growth of cotton. Hailstorms take a big toll in the cotton belt. Lack of rainfall may retard planting or impair the germination of cotton seed. Little moisture and high winds may cause the seed to sprout and then to dry out. Strong winds may cause extensive physical damage to a cotton crop. A cold, wet spring may cause widespread cutworm damage, while the cotton aphid prefers cold nights and hot days to be most active. The fruiting and flowering of the cotton plant is a complicated process which is particularly vulnerable to climate. Often a cotton plant aborts during the fruiting stage, or as the young bolls are formed if the weather conditions are not compatible. Abortion will occur when high temperatures result in high transpiration and low soil moisture, when heavy rains occur, when sudden changes in weather occur, such as wet to dry, cloudy to clear, and cool to hot. The boll weevil is an ever-present threat to the cotton crop, and if weather conditions favor the boll weevil's life cycle, then a cotton crop will be devastated. The economic value of cotton depends upon the color, the luster, the quality of the fiber, and the amount of dirt in the boll. These qualities depend critically upon the weather during the formation and growth of the boll. Cotton picked shortly after the opening of the boll is bright and creamy, but if it is picked after long exposure to the sun, it will be dull and blue. Careless harvesting practices result in enormous economic losses to cotton farmers. Weather conditions are critical at almost every stage of development of a cotton crop right through to harvesting and ginning. If the cotton bale is stored or handled badly, then excess moisture can cause rapid deterioration of the quality of the fibers.

Tobacco grows best when the mean air temperature is about 26.6°C (80°F) during the growing season, and leaves of tobacco burn when air temperatures exceed about 35°C (95°F). Tobacco plants are usually started in cold frames or hotbeds, where they are nurtured for six to ten weeks before being set out in the field. Cottonseeds require temperatures of 23.9°C (75°F) to 26.7°C (80°F) for the best germination and are killed if their temperatures exceed 35°C (95°F). Tobacco requires 100-120 days for full maturity. Hence, it is necessary to make the most of the growing season in order to avoid frost at the end, but, since warm temperatures are required for germination, it is critical to begin the plants in cold frames or hotbeds and to put them outside as early as safe weather conditions permit. Tobacco plants require fairly uniform water availability throughout the season, and too much water causes waterlogged soils or fungal diseases.

Wheat, rye, oats, barley, and other small grains grow best where the annual precipitation is not less than 15 in. per year and does not exceed 30 in. per year. When rainfall is heavy, say 45 in. per year or more, it is not so much the excess water that hurts the crop as the indirect effects of rust, mildew, and other pathogens. These small grain crops are quite resistant to cold and are seeded as early in the spring as possible, often emerging as young plants before the last killing frost. Cold hardening is essential for winter wheat to survive the winter. The process of cold hardening is one in which the plant is subjected to gradually colder weather. During this period the water content of its sap diminishes, the amount of free water in its tissues decreases, and the sugar content increases. If a very cold period in late November or early December is preceded by a week or two of unseasonably warm weather, then winter kill of small grain will occur. Plants seem to decrease in cold hardiness during late winter and early spring when severe cold can result in much kill. As the winter wheat crop comes into head in the spring it flowers, pollen fertilizes the flowers, and grain develops. If the weather is suddenly cold at this stage, the pollen is killed and fertilization will not occur. On the other hand, if the weather becomes too warm during the heading and ripening stages, a hot wind can desiccate the plants and reduce yield considerably. Low or high soil moisture during the autumn planting of winter wheat also affects yields. The quality of grain, in particular the protein content, is acutely affected by weather. Since nitrogen is an essential compound for protein synthesis, the effect of weather on protein content must be through the nitrogen cycle, the amount and form of nitrogen in the soil, and its absorption by the plants.

Climate or weather affects crops in almost every conceivable manner. The climate may influence the biochemistry and physiological processes of plant growth directly through temperature and light, or by affecting germination or fertilization. Indirectly, climate influences growth by affecting heat resistance and cold hardiness, the nitrogen, phosphorus, potassium, and other mineral cycles, or by affecting the plant through water logging of soil, leaching of minerals from soil, or by affecting the oxygen uptake from the soil. Climate influences growth even more indirectly by affecting the activity of a plant pathogen, such as rust or mildew, by influencing an insect population, and finally, by interfering with the cultivation and harvesting of the crop.

viruses

Most viruses infecting plants are transmitted by insects. The primary exception to this is the tobacco mosaic virus, which is highly infectious and easily transmitted by direct contact. Climate affects the insect transmitting a virus as well as the vigor, condition, and distribution of the crop which may be liable to infection. Viruses spread most rapidly when climate conditions are best for insect multiplication and migration. Aphids and leafhoppers are the main vectors for plant viruses. Aphids multiply at the greatest rate when the temperature is about 26.1°C

138

*man
and his
environment:
climate*

(79°F). As a result, aphid populations and the transmittal of
viruses to plants is greatest when summers are warm and in
warm continental regions. As temperatures rise, the aphid life
cycle shortens, and it is possible to produce more generations
during a season. Usually warmer climates are the more southern climates in the Northern Hemisphere, and consequently
they have longer growing seasons. In these southern climates
larger population densities and more generations of aphids will
occur than in northern regions. As a result, there is a greater
likelihood of virus transmittal and infection to crops. Striking
differences in aphid populations are seen between southern
England, where potato aphids may pass through four generations in a season, and Scotland, where only three generations
will occur. Furthermore, in the warmer climates the aphids are
more active and more likely to be transported from one site to
another. Winged aphids do not fly when air temperatures are
less than about 13.3°C (56°F). Their activity increases as temperatures increase to about 30°C (86°F). At higher temperatures aphid activity begins to diminish. Hence, in South Africa,
where the mean daily temperature is above 31.7°C (89°F),
aphids no longer infest potatoes. When daytime temperatures
are around 26.7°C (80°F) to 29.4°C (85°F), aphids are very
active, moving frequently from one part of a crop to another,
and the resulting virus infection can be very serious indeed.
Agronomists will attempt to take advantage of these situations. For example, lettuce is grown for seed in hot climates of
Australia and California, where the aphid activity is minimal
and the transmittal of the lettuce mosaic virus is reduced. We
should remind ourselves that light is particularly important to
aphid activity. Aphids do not fly in the dark, and during the
daylight hours very substantial differences in aphid movement
occur in full sunshine, cloudiness, and dawn or dusk conditions. Often just a single cloud over the sun will cause a sudden
drop of aphid movement.

Temperature not only affects the disease vectors, but it affects the virus infectiousness. The aster yellow virus loses infectiousness after 12 days at temperatures of about 32.2°C
(90°F). As a result, in the United States this virus causes more

damage in cool weather late in the season than during the hot summer, but fortunately the aster plants are more resistant to the virus late in the season, and the transmittal vectors are fewer. This is a good example of the truly complex relations which operate within communities of organisms and physical environments. By contrast to the aster yellow virus the potato leaf roll virus is spread by a vector which is more active at high temperatures than at low temperatures, just at the time when the potato plant is more susceptible to infection. The consequence is more serious infection and damage of potato plants during warm weather than during cool weather.

Heavy rain will wash the insect vectors from the plants and cause their death and a reduction of disease. On the other hand, wet weather may cause abundant growth of a crop or plant community as well as a commensurate increase of the insect vectors feeding on the plants. An insect vector will often live and breed in a natural community of grasses and shrubs, then at some propitious moment he will move to a nearby crop. Such is the case in Colorado with a leafhopper, which carries the curly top virus of beets. These leafhoppers live among the weeds and grasses in the foothills of the Rockies during the winter and move into the beet fields of the cultivated valleys and plains during the summer. The virus is actually resident in some of the weed plants of the semiarid foothills. The leafhoppers feed on these plants, become infected, and carry the virus to the beets. During wet years the plants harboring the virus grow abundantly, and the rate of infection by the migrating leafhoppers is much greater than during sparse, dry years.

The structure and density of a crop affects the microclimate among the plants. A dense crop will have a dark, cool interior with much of the sunlight reflected from the uppermost foliage of transpiring leaves. The interior of a dense crop is relatively still without much wind being able to penetrate the upper layers of leaves. An open crop is sunlit, warm, and more windy. The incident sunlight dries out the soil surface, making the surface hotter than when it is moist and shaded. Sunlight reflects to the leaves, where it is absorbed, and the leaves get warm, in turn warming the air within them. These differences of temperature, moisture, and windiness between open and closed crop canopies can be crucial to the spread of plant diseases by insect vectors. Small insects can navigate to where they wish to go only when wind levels are low. Although aphids and other small insects are carried great distances by strong winds, they must get near the ground where wind speeds are reduced in order to home in on the proper host. Usually the plants along the edge of a crop will be infected first, and then the viral disease will spread on into the interior of the crop. In this context the reader should remind himself of the wind profile which exists above a rough surface. The wind speed diminishes to zero at the surface itself and increases above the surface in a manner proportional to the roughness of the surface. The wind speed will increase more slowly with height above a forest or crop than above a meadow or flat surface. Near the top of the crop or trees the air flow will be turbulent and irregular, with both horizontal and vertical movement at once. This mixing of the air will cause the crop to "breathe" as air is exchanged between the interior and the free flow above the crop surface. The temperature at all locations within a crop will be affected by this exchange of air. Also affected will be the activity and migration of insect vectors, as well as the virulence of the crop pathogens.

energy budget of plants

One of the best ways to understand the effect of climate on plants is to understand the exchange of energy between a plant and its environment. If the air is cooler than the plant, as is often the case, then the only significant heat input to a plant is from the incident radiation which is absorbed. If the air is warmer than the plant, then some heat energy enters the plant by means of convection. As with everything else, a plant must remain in energy balance in order to survive. It cannot absorb more energy than it gets rid of, or it will become progressively hotter. A plant cannot lose more energy than it absorbs over an extended period of time, or it will become progressively colder. Using the principle of energy balance, we can account for the influence of climate on plant temperature and on transpiration or water loss rate.

A leaf will absorb an amount of incident radiation from the environment, including direct sunlight, reflected sunlight, scattered skylight, and infrared radiant heat. This absorbed energy will raise the leaf temperature to a temperature T and will also vaporize a certain amount of water within the leaf. This vapor will escape through the open pores or stomates into the drier air beyond the boundary layer adhering to the leaf surface. This process of transpiration of water vaporizing and escaping we have discussed earlier. Every gram of water which is converted to vapor requires approximately 580 cal of energy. Hence, the transpiration process itself acts like an evaporative cooler in the same manner as the evaporative coolers which are used in many homes. A leaf will be cooler as a result of transpiration.

If the air is cooler than the leaf itself, then the flow of air across the leaf surface will pick up heat from the leaf and carry away a definite amount of energy by means of convection. Whenever there is air movement because of wind near a leaf, there is an exchange of energy. Even when there is no wind there is air movement around a leaf if there is a temperature difference between the leaf and the air, and energy is transferred by the natural process of convection. If the air is warmer than the leaf, then there is energy transferred from the air to the leaf by convection. The amount of energy transferred to or from a leaf surface by convection is proportional to the difference in temperature between the leaf and the air, but the amount of energy transferred also varies directly with the square root of the wind speed, and inversely with the square root of the width of the leaf. The larger the leaf is, the thicker is the boundary layer of air which adheres to the leaf surface. Therefore, the rate at which heat is transferred to or from the leaf by convection is inversely proportional to the size of the leaf. The inverse proportion happens to be, for a flat plate-like object, such as a leaf, according to the square root of the dimension. For objects of other shapes, such as cylinders and spheres, the power function is different in each case.

If a leaf surface absorbs a total amount of radiation R and if the only way a leaf could get rid of this energy was by reradiation according to the blackbody law of radiation, then for energy balance we could write:

Energy in = Energy out

$$R = \sigma T^4 \tag{9}$$

Here $\sigma = 8.13 \times 10^{-11}$ cal cm^{-2} °K^{-4} min^{-1} and T is in degrees Kelvin when R is in calories per square centimeter per minute. When using the blackbody formula with T^4, absolute temperature must always be used.

In this simple balance of energy the only environmental factor which influences the leaf is the amount of radiation received by the leaf from the environment and the absorptivity of the leaf surface to the incident radiation. Both of the factors are contained implicitly in R. The temperature, wind speed, and humidity of the air have nothing to do with the energy balance of a leaf in the context assumed here, and the leaf temperature relates directly and simply to the amount of radiation absorbed by the leaf. In order to compare the leaf temperatures under this circumstance with those which result when convection and transpiration are included, we refer to the values given in Table 12. It is noticed that if the amount of

table 12
**leaf temperatures in degrees centigrade
for the conditions listed**

R (cal cm^{-2} min^{-1})	radiation only	radiation and convection V (cm sec^{-1})			radiation, convection, and transpiration V (cm sec^{-1})		
		10	100	500	10	100	500
0.6	20	28	29	30	25	27	29
1.0	60	41	34	32	33	31	30
1.4	89	53	39	34	40	35	32

radiation absorbed by the leaf is 0.6 cal cm^{-2} min^{-1} and if the leaf cools by reradiation only, the leaf temperature is 20°C (68°F); if $R = 1.0$ cal cm^{-2} min^{-1}, $T = 333$°K or 60°C (130°F); and if $R = 1.4$ cal cm^{-2} min^{-1}, $T = 362$°K or 89°C (193°F). In other words, if an object, such as a leaf, could lose the radiation it absorbed by emitting it as radiation from its surface, it would become very warm even for ordinary amounts of energy absorbed.

If a leaf loses energy by radiation and by convection, we can write the energy balance in the following form:

Energy in = Energy out

$$R = \sigma T^4 + 6 \times 10^{-3} \sqrt{V/D} \ (T - T_a) \tag{10}$$

where V is the wind speed in centimeters per second, D is the width of leaf in centimeters, and T_a is the air temperature in degrees centigrade. The value of T in the T^4 term must be used in degrees Kelvin, but wherever differences of temperature occur, such as $T - T_a$, both T and T_a can be in degrees centigrade. Now we see that two new environmental factors, i.e., wind speed and air temperature, enter the energy balance relation. Just by adding the convection term we find that radiation, wind speed, and air temperature simultaneously affect the temperature of the leaf. The environment or climate becomes a three-dimensional proposition. We can no longer discuss the influence of a certain amount of radiation incident upon a leaf without discussing simultaneously the air temperature and wind speed. Nor can we talk about a certain amount of radiation and a given air temperature without considering the wind speed. In this formulation we consider that a wind speed of 10 cm sec^{-1} is equivalent to no air movement. Clearly if V is set equal to zero the convection term will go to zero. This cannot be allowed since we know that some convection, we call it free or natural convection, occurs even in still air, and so we arbitrarily select a lower limit which can be used for the value of V. If we were to discuss this more accurately, we would need to go into detail concerning the entire subject of free and forced convection.

If we put in the same amount of absorbed radiation as before, we now get lower leaf temperatures, since some energy is being lost by convection. Table 12 shows the leaf temperature in the case of energy loss by radiation plus convection when the air temperature is 30°C (86°F). Now at a high amount of absorbed radiation, 1.4 cal cm^{-2} min^{-1}, which is typical of full sunshine at noon on a clear day, the leaf temperature in still air drops from its value of 89°C (192°F) with radiation only to 53°C (127°F), and in wind it drops to a value of 100 cm sec^{-1} (2.2 mph) and 500 cm sec^{-1} (11 mph) to 39°C (102°F) and 34°C (93°F), respectively. For the case of low amounts of absorbed radiation, e.g., 0.6 cal cm^{-2} min^{-1}, which is typical of the amount of radiation absorbed on a warm night, the leaf temperature increases in still air to 28°C (82°F) and to 29°C (84°F) and 30°C (86°F) in wind of 100 cm sec^{-1} and 500 cm sec^{-1}, respectively, compared to its value of 20°C (68°F) when cooled by radiation only. The increase in temperature occurs because the air is warmer than the leaf (the air temperature is 30°C) and heat is delivered to the leaf by convective heat transfer. These numbers illustrate the enormous importance to leaf temperatures of the presence of air and the effectiveness of convection as an energy transfer mechanism. Without the action of convection leaves would simply denature and dry up.

If we add the ability to cool by transpiration, we see from Table 12 that leaf temperatures are reduced further in all cases. In fact, in still air the reduction is 13°C over that of cooling by radiation and convection only when the amount of radiation absorbed is 1.4 cal cm^{-2} min^{-1}, while at 100 cm sec^{-1} (2.2 mph) the reduction of leaf temperature is only 4°C and at 500 cm sec^{-1} (11 mph) it is 2°C. At low amounts of absorbed radiation, the leaf temperature, which increased when convection was involved in addition to energy exchange by radiation, only now decreased with transpirational cooling. The energy budget equation involving transpiration in addition to radiation and convection is written:

$$R = \sigma T^4 + 6 \times 10^{-3} \sqrt{V/D}\,(T - T_a) + 580\,\frac{{}_s d_\varrho - \text{rh}\;{}_s d_a}{r_\varrho + r_a} \quad (11)$$

where $_sd_\varrho$ and $_sd_a$ are the saturation concentrations of water vapor in grams per cubic centimeter in the leaf and in the air, respectively, and rh is the relative humidity of the air, expressed as a decimal fraction. Although the latent heat of vaporization depends upon the temperature, we shall take here, for a first approximation, its value at 30°C of 580 cal g^{-1}. The internal resistance of the leaf to water loss is r_ϱ and the resistance introduced by the boundary layer adhering to the leaf surface is r_a, each measured in minutes per centimeter. The internal resistance used for calculating Table 12 is 2 sec cm^{-2}, which is equivalent to 0.033 min cm^{-1}. This is a relatively low internal resistance, but not as low as for some agronomic plants where the internal diffusion resistance is 1.0 sec cm $^{-1}$ or less.

Equation (11) gives us the opportunity of seeing for a plant the manner in which the four independent climate variables of radiation absorbed, air temperature, wind speed, and humidity affect a plant. These independent climate variables affect directly the dependent variables of leaf temperature and transpiration rate and indirectly the rates of photosynthesis and respiration. We know now with precision just how wind speed affects leaf temperature and water loss in the context of any given amount of radiation and values of air temperature and relative humidity. We know exactly the leaf temperature and water loss rate as a function of the air temperature and the relative humidity for a fixed amount of wind and radiation for a specific plant with particular properties. All of these answers are achieved from the solution of Eq. (11).

Photosynthesis depends upon the diffusion of carbon dioxide into the leaf through the stomates and through the mesophyll cell walls to the chloroplasts. However, the rate of CO_2 diffusion must be compatible with the rate at which the carbon dioxide is used up, in the manufacturing process of photosynthesis within the chloroplasts, less the rate at which carbon dioxide is released by respiration, from the peroxyzomes of the mesophyll cells in the leaf. The rate at which the manufacturing process of carbohydrates occurs is temperature and light dependent as well as dependent on the concentration of carbon dioxide available. The temperature dependence of photosynthesis is very similar to the curve shown in Fig. 13 in which there is an optimum temperature for the greatest rate of reaction. The dependence of photosynthesis on light and carbon dioxide concentration is in the form of a linear increase at low values, which then slows down at intermediate values, and approaches a limiting rate of photosynthesis at high values of light and carbon dioxide. Climate is intimately tied to plant response through these mechanisms.

These kinetic rate processes of the biochemistry of the leaf are regulated by enzymes within the leaf and account for a great deal of the environmental response of a plant, and also for such adaptation to climate and habitat, as is observed in phenotypic-ecotypic variation of plants throughout the world. Why some plant species grow well on mountain tops, in the arctic tundra, on the prairies, in the north woods, in the tropical forest, or on a coral atoll is one of the great unanswered questions concerning the living world. In order to realize the answer to this question we must understand the complete plant in a holistic manner which includes the biochemistry, physiology, anatomy, ecology, and systematics of the plant and the physical environment in which it grows.

6
climate
change
and
pollution

climate modification

Man's activities in industry and transportation are so enormous, so constant, and so widespread over the earth that the pollutants entering the atmosphere are threatening potential global changes of climate. The most difficult questions to be answered are: Precisely what changes of climate are occurring, if any, and what are the specific causes? There are, of course, natural changes of climate, both local and global, which have occurred since time immemorial. There is much conjecture as to the causes of these natural changes, whether they are due to variations of the solar output of radiation; differences in aspect of the earth in orbit around the sun due to nutation, the movement of the earth on its axis like the nodding of a top, or oscillation, changes from the earth's magnetic field; variations of atmospheric transmission by volcanic dust; or simply changes caused by the interactions of the atmosphere, oceans, and icecaps.

Changes which occur naturally have generally a long time span, evolving over hundreds or even thousands of years. Human population since the industrial revolution has exploded and spread across all land masses, and with it a proliferation of industry, transportation, and agriculture, which is so massive and so continuous that the limitations of the planet earth are now being realized. The input of particulates and chemicals to the atmosphere is so enormous that the atmosphere can no longer cleanse itself and climatic changes may result.

The industrial revolution began only 200 years ago, but industrialization required the burning of enormous amounts of fossil fuels. The by-products of combustion are water vapor, carbon dioxide, carbon monoxide, oxides of sulfur, and other undesirable minor constituents, all of which are released into the atmosphere. Although forests and grasslands have burned naturally ever since they first grew upon the earth, and although man had long set fires for warmth, for agricultural purposes, and to facilitate cooking of game, the massive consumptive burning of fossil fuels has added a new dimension to the input of by-products of combustion into our atmosphere.

Perhaps we should begin our discussion of inadvertent climate change by taking a look at what has happened to the mean temperature of the Northern Hemisphere during the last nearly 100 years. Figure 16 illustrates dramatically why we are concerned with what has happened. Beginning at about 1880 there was a definite warming trend until about 1940. During this 60-year interval the mean temperature of the Northern Hemisphere increased by $1.0°F$ or about $0.6°C$. During this same period the carbon dioxide concentration of the atmosphere increased by about 11%. This apparent coincidence has suggested that the warming of the atmosphere during this period was the result of the *greenhouse effect* of CO_2 in the atmosphere. The term "greenhouse" is somewhat of a misnomer, but, nevertheless, it is used in the context that carbon dioxide gas in the atmosphere is transparent to incoming sunlight, but somewhat opaque to long-wave infrared radiation. The reason for this is that the carbon dioxide molecule has a strong absorption band centered about a wavelength of 4.3μ in the infrared portion of the spectrum and another centered at about 14.0μ. A blackbody radiator at the mean temperature of the earth's surface, $289°K$, emits infrared radiation with a

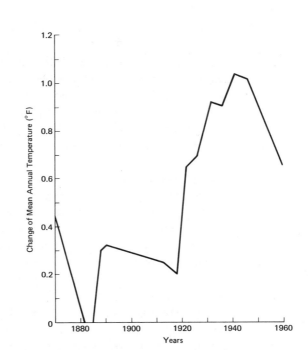

figure 16. *Change of the mean annual temperature of the Northern Hemisphere from 1875 to 1960.*

broad distribution of wavelengths, but with peak emission at a wavelength of about $10\,\mu$. Carbon dioxide, with broad absorption bands on either side of $10\,\mu$, interacts with the outgoing stream of radiation from the earth's surface. It absorbs some of the radiation and then emits this energy in two directions, i.e., upward and downward. It also emits at an average temperature much lower than $289°$K. The result is a reduction of the total amount of radiant energy which would pass out into space if the earth's surface radiated freely through a totally transparent atmosphere. Careful calculations show that for an increase of carbon dioxide concentration of 11%, about a $0.5°$C ($0.9°$F) rise of the mean temperature of the Northern Hemisphere could be expected. This does not say that the increase in carbon dioxide concentration was indeed the causative agent, but it does suggest it is probable.

Measurements made during a period of several years, about 1958 or so, at the Pole Station, at Little America in Antarctica, and on Mauna Loa in Hawaii of the carbon dioxide concentration indicate an average increase of carbon dioxide concentration in the atmosphere of about 0.7 ppm (parts per million) a year. The normal concentration of carbon dioxide is about 315 ppm, but this varies a great deal with locale and with time of day. The daytime concentrations are reduced considerably (250 ppm or less) because of photosynthesis drawing in carbon dioxide to the green plants, and the nighttime concentrations reach 400 ppm or more near the surface because of respiration from plants and animals and the absence of photosynthesis at night. The interesting aspect of the measurements mentioned above is that they were made at stations far removed from sources of industrial contamination. The Mauna Loa measurements were made at a station located on the lava-laden slope of the mountain above the tree limit, and the dense tropical forests were all far below. Nevertheless the diurnal effect of photosynthesis and respiration by the forest vegetation was clearly evident in the records. Despite this diurnal influence, the rate of increase of carbon dioxide concentration averaged out to the same figure as that obtained in Antarctica. Actually, the total amount of carbon dioxide released to the atmosphere by the burning of fossil fuels is more than double the amount which the atmosphere seems to have gained. The question is: Where has it all gone? It is likely that more carbon has been bound up in carbohydrates by the assimilation process of green plants. Photosynthesis or productivity is directly proportional to the atmospheric concentration of carbon dioxide at the present levels of concentration. Hence, an increase of atmospheric carbon dioxide will result in a direct increase of productivity and more carbon bound into the products of assimilation.

Some people have calculated that industrial effluents cannot be the primary source of the carbon dioxide concentration increase in the atmosphere, but that, in fact, it is from the slow oxidation of peat bogs or the slash-and-burn agriculture still practiced in clearing fields in many parts of the world. In the latter instance it would still be caused by man. It is just possible that the increased CO_2 (carbon dioxide) concentration is the result of the warming trend, seen in Fig. 16, rather than the cause of it; i.e., the warming produces an increase of respiration from plants and the release of more carbon dioxide from the oceans. It just goes to show how complicated the earth–atmosphere system is, how subtle are the causes and effects, and how very difficult it is to be sure of anything.

We notice from Fig. 16 that an abrupt cooling trend set in about 1940, and that the mean temperature of the Northern Hemisphere has been cooling ever since. Why this should be we do not know. We can speculate only. We believe it possible that the increased pollution from industry and automobiles, combined with the prevalence of jet contrails in the sky, is changing the transparency of the atmosphere, causing increased sunlight to be reflected back into space, less radiation to reach the ground, and a cooler resulting ground surface and atmosphere. An increase of 30% per decade of the turbidity over Mauna Loa Observatory, far from sources of pollution, has been noted. An increase of 3–4% turbidity, averaged over the earth, appears to be adequate to lower the global temperature by 0.3–0.5°C (0.5–0.9°F). The increased turbidity of the air above the Rocky Mountains and the Alps, each far removed from pollution, seems to be of about this order of magnitude.

Jet contrails lace the skies of the world by the thousands per day and produce sufficient seeding of cirrus clouds to have some influence on the global radiation balance of the planet. Very often, when skies would normally be clear, the jet contrails spread out into the blue and form persistent amounts of cirrus clouds which reflect sunlight back to space.

We really do not know what is going on. We do not know positively what is *cause* and what is *effect*. All we believe is that something may be happening. There may be a warming trend because of continuing increase of carbon dioxide concentration in the atmosphere and there may be a cooling trend because of increased turbidity caused by dustiness and pollution generally. The really frightening thing is that something man-made may indeed be affecting the global system of land, sea, and air which will result in a worldwide change of climate.

Frits Went, the famous physiologist who discovered plant auxin, a substance which promotes plant growth by cell elongation and causes root formation and bud inhibition, decided a few years ago to establish the origin of the persistent blue hazes which have existed in the atmosphere, particularly during the autumn months, or more often, over such regions as the Blue Ridge Mountains of Virginia. He showed that during the autumn, when leaves are dying and falling from the trees, large amounts of *terpenes*, which are volatile organic substances, are released into the air. Among the aerosols released, only certain ones have an odor which is noticed by people. It happens that a pine forest emits a higher percentage of aromatic aerosols than does an oak forest, although they both emit about the same total amount of aerosols. Approximately 4.4×10^8 tons of aerosols per year are ejected by the forests of the world into the atmosphere. Some people have suggested that the pollution by man is inconsequential, in terms of its effect on the global climate, in comparison with the amounts of aerosols released by plants into the atmosphere. However, man's pollution is of a new character and is rapidly increasing in quantity. The aerosols, dust, and chemicals released by industry could create serious changes of the earth's climate. Furthermore, man's pollutants are released all the time even during seasons of the year when the aerosols from forests may be at a minimum.

Vincent Schaefer, the scientist who invented the method of artificially seeding clouds by the use of dry ice, has suggested that the particulate matter introduced into the atmosphere by pollution is in fact causing a substantial change of the character of clouds formed and the rainfall pattern in the Adirondacks. He suggests that the persistent particulate matter ejected into the sky is seeding the moisture, prematurely causing increased mist and not allowing the usual thermal buildup of thunderstorms. Very often falling mist evaporates before reaching the ground, whereas the larger, heavier droplets of thunderstorms do fall to earth. Hence, precipitation as mist may be completely ineffective at the surface, while the thunderstorm will wet it well. The reasoning behind this idea is the fact that water vapor in the air, in order to form droplets of water, requires nuclei upon which to condense, or droplet formation requires instead the dynamics of a thunderstorm, within which the electrical fields assist the droplets with coalescence, as they become larger and fall out as rain. It was the discovery of the process of nucleation which led Vincent Schaefer to try seeding of supersaturated air by dry ice particles in a cold chamber to form ice crystals and snowflakes. A colleague of Schaefer's, Bernard Vonnegut, then discovered that very small crystals of silver iodide had the proper crystal structure to be effective nuclei for the formation of ice or snow crystals. An enormous amount of effort and money has been spent during the last twenty years on rainmaking projects whereby moisture-laden air masses are seeded with silver iodide from fuel burning generators on the ground.

I was with Schaefer and Vonnegut one winter in Yellowstone National Park studying processes of cloud formation and ecological events near the thermal hot springs along the Firehole River near Old Faithful Geyser. One night with the air temperature about $-15°C$ ($5°F$) and the ground covered with three feet of snow, I left them working at Old Faithful. I went about a mile below in the valley, where I was measuring the temperatures of plants living near some of the hot springs. It was a crystal clear, sparkling, cold night. The stars stood out like pinpoints in the sky, and the Milky Way was a corridor of starlight in the sky. Suddenly, out of this clear sky, it began to snow and the most exquisite blanket of fine snow crystals began to coat the surface. I was at first surprised, and then I realized that my colleagues had probably fired up their silver iodide generators, sending billions of tiny crystals into the sky to form condensation nuclei for the abundant moisture of the supersaturated air from the hot springs. It was now overcast, no longer could I see the starlight, and the gentle snowstorm continued to fall.

Cloud seeding has been used by the Air Force to open up fog-bound airstrips. By flying just over the fog or clouds and dumping out finely divided particles of dry ice, it is possible to cause nucleation and precipitation to create a clear opening through the clouds in order to permit planes to land. Some of the larger civilian airlines have demonstrated a 5:1 benefit commercially, and many plane landings and takeoffs do occur now that otherwise would not in the absence of cloud seeding. In one experiment 11 lb of dry ice produced a hole in the clouds more than 3 miles wide and a couple of miles long in 1 h. Cloud seeding with silver iodide has been used extensively in northern Italy and some in the Soviet Union to attempt to generate rainfall and fallout from hailstorms in order to avert the normal buildup of large hailstones. The technique was partially successful and some savings to agriculture were achieved. Hail damage to crops was reduced three to five times in some of the experiments reported from the Soviet Union. The first successful attempt to seed hurricanes, and to sap their strength before they reach full intensity, was achieved in 1961. Recent seeding of hurricanes in the Gulf of Mexico has met with moderate success. Hurricane Debbie in 1969 was seeded while she was still out at sea. The results appeared to be highly satisfactory. Hurricane Debbie remained at sea, only brushing by Bermuda and Newfoundland, and failed to gain her full potential fury.

Experiments to seed rain clouds in order to increase precipitation are somewhat inconclusive. There is evidence that rainfall can be increased from 10 to 20% when seeding is done under precisely the proper conditions. Moisture must be present, and the clouds must be ripe for seeding. There is considerable question as to whether or not increased precipitation over one region implies a reduction of precipitation somewhere else. This raises the interesting legal question as to who has title to the water passing over private land. It would seem that our cities are inadvertently seeding the air and modifying their climates and climates of other areas all the time.

During the next few decades we should see considerable advances in the techniques of modifying weather on a local basis, with definitive benefits to agriculture, transportation, and commerce. Progress with respect to large-scale weather modification will be slower, but some advances in this domain can be expected. The vexing question still remains as to how much large-scale inadvertent weather modification or climate change will continue to occur as the result of man's continued use of the ocean of air as a massive dilutant to his emission products, or even to what degree man can willfully modify the climate for his own convenience.

climates of cities

When man builds a house or a building, the climate outside in the vicinity of the structure is modified immediately. The south wall of the house reflects sunlight, and the building reduces any wind movement from the north, with the result that the area around the southern exposure is hotter and drier than it was without the building. At the same time the ground adjacent to the north wall of the house is colder, less sunny, and wetter than it was before the presence of the building. The ground near the east-facing wall will be protected from the prevailing westerlies. It will receive intense morning sun but will have sunset at about noon. The ground near the west-facing wall will have sunrise at about noon, a normal sunset, will receive the full impact of the hottest part of the day, and the wall itself will remain warm into the evening hours while it radiates heat to the ground and sky.

A single building affects the radiation regime of the adjacent areas by drastically changing the hours of either sunrise or sunset or both and by acting as a blackbody radiator at the temperature of the wall. The building will interfere with the wind pattern, so that there may result a windy side and a protected side with an occasional eddy swirling into it. Snow accumulation is affected dramatically by a building; the windward side remains relatively free of snow, and snow accumulation forms on the leeward side. Snow accumulation near the north wall of a building will last far beyond any accumulation near the south wall, and the winter climate of the north wall will, seemingly, last weeks longer than that of the south wall. Depending on the location of drainpipes and downspouts, the moisture regime may be very wet in certain areas (often the corners) and relatively dry or normal in other areas. The total precipitation onto the roof is funneled into these few wet spots, which may receive 10–100 times the normal amount of precipitation.

Two buildings near one another will create most of the phenomena described above, but, in addition, if they are relatively close together, they may have between them an alley of much wind, since it acts as a funnel, little sunshine, and much moisture if the downspouts drain the rainfall there. If the alleyway between the buildings runs east and west, and is of sufficient width, the sun will fall directly into the area and be reflected between the two walls to create a radiation regime of great intensity. Usually the walls of Spanish houses are whitewashed to reflect the sunshine in order to reduce heat absorption by the wall. The alleyway or courtyard between the buildings may be brilliant with reflected sunshine and unbearably hot to any plant or animal located there. T. E. Lawrence (Lawrence of Arabia) wrote: "Do not fall into the Khartoum fault of wide streets; in the Tropics air is an enemy, also sunlight." Indeed this is so, for the sun is very high in the sky most of the year in the tropics and will beat down into any courtyard or alleyway. Some tropical cities will have very narrow streets and passageways so that they are partially shaded and relatively cool.

Life forms near a building or buildings are strongly indicative of the climate in the vicinity of each wall. Insects will emerge early in the spring along the south wall; plants will emerge first and bloom earliest there; birds will feed in its protective warmth; and in early spring people will sunbathe or relax in the sun along a southern wall. Skiers bask in the southern exposure of a resort lodge and enjoy the warmth of snow-reflected sunshine. During the warm summer months the southern exposure is hot, dry, and unbearable to many organisms, while the northern wall will find birds in its shade, insects in profusion, and plants blooming and growing well. An interior courtyard within one building, or enclosed by several buildings, experiences a unique protective climate of warmth and comfort during the winter, but such a sunlit, windless courtyard is often unbearably hot during the summer.

A small village on windswept plains or a cluster of houses high in the Alps creates an amazing change of climate between and among the buildings. Small children play in the sunshine protected from the wind in the lee of the buildings, and dogs sleep by the baseboards. As a village becomes a town, and a town evolves into a city, many substantial and more pervading changes of climate occur. We now know that a city is dirtier, warmer, rainier, cloudier, less sunny, and less windy than the nearby countryside.

A city of stone and concrete structures and black asphalt paving is a hearthstone of heat, as sunlight is reflected time and again among the buildings to be absorbed by their walls. During the winter months furnaces warm the walls from within. Because of the massive amounts of air conditioning required during the summer, every air conditioner expels additional plumes of heat into the hot summer air. Many of us know well the uncomfortable experience of the heat emitted from a west-facing wall during a summer evening. The concrete walls of a city store a great deal of heat during a summer day, and therefore they radiate warmth for many evening hours. The concrete walls store more heat during daylight hours than a bare soil surface, and in turn they lose the heat at a faster rate during the evening. When sunlight falls on a forest, or on soil, most of the radiation absorbed is stored in the uppermost layers of the plant growth or ground. By contrast, the walls of the city reflect sunlight and heat, thereby absorbing it over a surface area which is very much more distributed than are the upper leaves of a canopy or the surface of the ground. The plants of the forest transpire and create evaporative cooling of the air around them, while the city has a surface of dryness with little opportunity for evaporative cooling.

The air of the city is linked dynamically with the air of the nearby countryside. The warm air of the city center fills with dirt and chemical pollutants from the factories and automobiles. This warm air rises forming a "dust dome" or "haze hood" over the city during the daylight hours. The warm, dirty air cools as it rises and sinks slowly toward the cooler country air at the perimeter, while at the same time the clean country air is being sucked toward the center of the city at the ground level. Whereas the dirty air of the "dust dome" at one time was confined primarily to the urban area, today it is becoming more ubiquitous, and the particulates of our urban atmospheres are being transported throughout the world.

At night the air above the city cools, and moisture condenses on nuclei of dust to form a mist or fog over the city. This blanket of water droplets above the city helps to screen radiational cooling from the city to space, while, at the same moment, the top of the "dust dome" cools radiatively, and the cooler air falls back into the city with its load of dust. Without strong wind or rain, the "dust dome" exaggerates itself day by day. A denser haze forms near the surface, and the population becomes choked and irritated by smog. Only when another front moves through the region does fresh air move into the city, flushing it free of smog and filth. Yet, just because the dirty air has moved out, we cannot ignore that it exists. This polluted city air is now graying the skies downwind, where it slowly becomes scrubbed of its particle load and pungent fumes.

Thus we see that the climate many miles downwind from cities is directly influenced and degraded by the filthy air of the great metropolitan areas. A classic example is La Porte, Indiana, 32 miles downwind from the steel mills of Chicago and Gary. La Porte has 38% more thunderstorms, 246% more hailstorms, 31% more rainfall, and considerably less sunshine than the neighboring countryside. Twenty percent of the thunderstorms in the region were in La Porte and nowhere else. The La Porte example is unique and receives the convergent influence of the steel mills and the moisture from Lake Michigan. The steel mills eject condensation nuclei, heat, and moisture into the air. Lake Michigan produces a dome of cold air above itself which acts as a barrier to the flow of the westerly or southwesterly winds which normally would disperse the air pollutants over the lake. Instead the pollutants, heat, and moisture are all channeled into a corridor headed directly over La Porte to the east. Violence ensues, and La Porte, Indiana, has a climate which is modified inadvertently by man.

Each city has its own personality and thereby has its own special climate; hence, it is difficult to infer the climate of all cities by generalizing from observations within one or a few cities. Yet, it seems eminently clear that cities are warmer, cloudier, dirtier, rainier, less sunny, and less humid than the surrounding countryside. There is evidence that cities of middle latitudes receive 15% less sunshine on horizontal surfaces than is received in nearby rural areas, 5% less ultraviolet radiation during summer months, and 30% less during the winter. The cities have 10% more cloudiness, 10% more precipitation, 25% lower mean annual wind speed, 30% more summer fog and 100% more winter fog, but curiously enough they have 6% lower annual mean relative humidity. The city air is often several degrees warmer than the country air. The first killing frost of the season in the country is often less severe in the city where the first killing frost may come days or even a week or so later. The average maximum temperature difference between city and countryside is about 3°C (5.4°F), but differences as great as 15°C (27°F) do occur.

air pollution

We would be remiss to discuss the urban climate and not describe the salient features of air pollution. The public has not only become aware of the presence of air pollution but is alarmed and concerned with the effects of pollution on human health and with the erosion of materials in the urban environment. Man has been using the atmosphere as a garbage dump, assuming it to be a vast, unbounded sea of air which would whisk away all debris dumped into it. Now he learns that the atmosphere is sharply confined to the troposphere, which extends from the ground to the stratosphere and contains 80% of the air. Man is beginning to discover that although brisk winds may take away his chimney smoke, he may be living downwind from a thousand other chimneys. He also learns that the wind does not always blow, and still air often prevails over his community for many days at a time, causing a rain of filth on him from above and a chemical stench every bit as bad as the decaying garbage must have been in the streets of a medieval city.

The evidence is now overwhelming that pollution affects the health of people living in large urban areas. The evidence comes from the statistics concerning morbidity and mortality, related to cancer, bronchitis, emphysema, and other serious diseases. The insidious aspect of such evidence is that we do not really notice directly how people are affected by air pollution, and it is often difficult for each of us living in cities to accept the fact that we may be a little less healthy than those living outside the urban pollution. Recent studies comparing the rates of emphysema in the population of St. Louis, Missouri, and Winnipeg, Canada, show the following: Among those who smoke cigarettes there is four times the incidence of emphysema in the St. Louis population as in the Winnipeg population, while among the nonsmokers the ratio is 10:1.

Donora, Pennsylvania, is a mining community located in the extremely narrow Monongahela River Valley, which is less than a mile wide with steep sides about 300 ft high. What happened here one day in 1948 is described by the following account: Tuesday morning of 26 October the weather was dead calm, cold, and cloudy. A dense fog closed in on the valley and the calm persisted through Wednesday and Thursday. One could scarcely see across the street as visibility was reduced by fog and smoke. The air had a sickening smell and reeked of sulfur dioxide. The mills, still spewing forth their effluents, had disappeared into the motionless mass of pollution. Approximately 43% of the inhabitants were made ill, about 65% of those over sixty-five years of age were affected, and about half of these were seriously ill. Twenty persons died as a direct result of the pollution, and, of these deaths, seventeen of them were during the third day of this invasion of pollution. The average, normal death rate and the usual variations from the norm are easily documented for a community.

The twenty additional deaths, over and above what might be expected, are definitely attributable to this episode.

Another case is the infamous smog episode in London, England, 5–8 December 1952. A stagnant air mass with temperature inversions settled over London, while millions of chimneys, thousands of automobiles and industries, and the huge power-generating plants all pumped their wastes directly into the atmosphere. There was no place for the pollutants to go except to "hang around." Visibility dropped, eyes smarted, people choked and coughed, and the life of this great city was attenuated. The number of deaths above normal for the week beginning during the smog episode was 2700, and the number of deaths remained considerably higher than normal for many weeks thereafter. Mortality increased among all ages of people, but the aged had by far the greatest incidence. Deaths were attributed to bronchitis, bronchopneumonia, and heart disease, all aggravated by pollution.

Those who fly frequently about the world are keenly aware of the vast numbers of pollution plumes which one sees in flight paths over New York, Chicago, Los Angeles, London, or any other great city. One realizes that the hackneyed phrase, "One man's pleasure is another man's poison," is really so true. The pollution of Chicago will stretch across Indiana, Michigan, and into Ohio. The foul air from Los Angeles is killing ponderosa pine trees in the San Bernardino Mountains 100 miles downwind from their points of origin, and pollution plume is evident as far to the east as Arizona. The pollution of Baltimore, Philadelphia, New York, and Boston will spread across the New England countryside when the wind is from the south or east. The prevailing westerlies normally will carry the air pollutants of this megalopolis out over the ocean, and one can pretend it doesn't matter. Or does it matter? Pilots flying jet aircraft out of north Africa bound for New York City report occasionally seeing the plume of blue-haze filth still persisting in the air over the Atlantic Ocean just off the west coast of Europe. There is no doubt that the air pollutants do not wash out within a few hundred miles of New York but ride with the air streams across the entire span of ocean. The particles are now becoming global "citizens," and the air, even in those parts of the world furthest removed from industrial contamination, is now dirty much of the time. The air above Mauna Loa in Hawaii is becoming less transparent at the rate of several percent per decade. On the sunniest days in Washington, D.C., the records at the Smithsonian Institution indicate about 16% less sunlight at the ground today than 40 or 50 years ago.

Table 13 gives an interesting comparison of the quality of urban air with normal rural air. What the table does not show are the maximum differences between urban and rural air, but the average amounts of those air pollutants which are the most damaging to human health, to plants, and to livestock. It is estimated that in 1966 approximately 29 million tons of sulfur dioxide were emitted into the atmosphere by all sources; 58% of this came from the combustion of coal, most of which was used to generate electrical power. The burning of fuel oil and other petroleum products accounted for 20%, while 6% came from the refining of petroleum, 12% from the smelting of sulfur-containing ores, 2% from sulfuric acid manufacturing, and the remaining 2% from all other sources. Concentrations of sulfur dioxide in the air of our cities often exceed 0.1 ppm by volume, and for short periods of an hour or less they may exceed 1.0 ppm. A concentration of 1.0 ppm by volume of sulfur dioxide is equivalent to 3000 $\mu g/m^3$ (micrograms per cubic meter). A person can taste concentrations of sulfur dioxide from 0.3 to 1.0 ppm (900 to 3000 $\mu g/m^3$). Sulfur

table 13
concentrations of air pollutants

pollutant	urban ($\mu g\ m^{-3}$)	rural ($\mu g\ m^{-3}$)
Sulfur dioxide	54	3
Nitrogen dioxide	59	2
Oxidant (ozone)	61	40
Carbon monoxide	4100	350
Methane	2800	810
Sulfates (SO_4)	11	0.5
Particulates	100	10

dioxide in the atmosphere is partly converted to sulfur trioxide or to sulfuric acid. The rate of oxidation of sulfur dioxide in the atmosphere depends upon the concentration of hydrocarbons, oxides of nitrogen, etc. The greatest amounts of atmospheric sulfur dioxide always occur where there is a large amount of burning of coal. Air pollution control agencies recommend the burning of coals only of low-sulfur content.

The primary effect of oxides of sulfur on human health is as an irritant to the respiratory system. Sulfur dioxide is shown to produce bronchoconstriction (contraction of the bronchial tubes of the lungs, causing difficulty in breathing) in experimental animals, such as the guinea pig. Studies of air pollution episodes in London suggest that a rise in the daily death rate occurred when the concentration of sulfur dioxide rose to 0.25 ppm ($715 \mu g/m^3$ in the presence of smoke at a density of $750 \mu g/m^3$). A more abrupt rise in deaths occurred when the concentrations exceeded 0.35 ppm ($1000 \mu g/m^3$) and smoke concentration reached $1200 \mu g/m^3$. A substantial amount of evidence now exists to show an increase of bronchitis, coughs, and other respiratory ailments as sulfur dioxide concentrations increase in the atmosphere. Generally people who are chronically ill have more serious effects from sulfur dioxide than healthy people. In addition, sulfur dioxide in the atmosphere causes serious corrosion of metals and other surfaces, and it can also cause severe damage to plants, resulting in leaf fall and diminished productivity. Sulfur dioxide in the air combines with water to form sulfuric acid fumes, and these cause runs in ladies' stockings. It is said that air pollutants have caused more deterioration of ancient statues in Rome in 20 years than had occurred previously in 2000 years.

The status of sulfur compounds in the global air is not well understood, nor are the sulfur cycles between ground and atmosphere. Yet we know that a large part of the sulfur in the global atmosphere is emitted as hydrogen sulfide from decaying organic matter on land and in the oceans, and also as gas emanating from volcanoes. In fact, at the present time, the amount of hydrogen sulfide contributed by industrial sources is not strongly significant on a global basis. However, local effects of hydrogen sulfide in the air can be very acute indeed when one is located near a source of hydrogen sulfide pollution.

The sulfur compounds, such as sulfur dioxide, hydrogen sulfide, sulfuric acid, and sulfate salts, when thrown into the atmosphere, return to earth one way or another. In the early 1960s the concentration of sulfur compounds in the air over some parts of Europe began to increase, as did the acidity of the rainfall. Normally rainfall is fairly neutral between an acid condition and an alkaline condition, but as moisture condenses in the atmosphere and falls as rain or snow, it absorbs sulfur compounds and other chemicals which are in the air, and the moisture becomes more acidic. In 1958 precipitation in Europe was only acidic occasionally over the Netherlands. By 1962 the areas of persistently acidic rainfall began to occur over central Europe, and by 1966 the rainfall over Sweden was becoming very acidic for the first time. Some of the lakes and waters of Sweden and northern Europe seem to be getting more acidic, which may be the result of more acidic rainfall. Most organisms cannot live in acidic waters. Therefore, a trend toward acidity in lakes and streams is a serious threat to their ecology. We may be seeing the beginning of such events, and if, as the result of continued buildup of industrial and power activity, more and more sulfur compounds enter the global air, we may see very serious disruption of the life cycles of water plants and animals. It is estimated that man-made activities contribute at the present time approximately one-third of the total input of sulfur compounds to the atmosphere, primarily as sulfur dioxide, but also some as hydrogen sulfide and other forms.

The normal atmosphere is made up of 78% nitrogen by volume, 21% oxygen, 1% argon, and other trace constituents. When combustion of fuel occurs, either in industrial or home furnaces, or in the internal combustion engines of automobiles, oxygen is consumed, water vapor, carbon monoxide, and carbon dioxide are produced, and other compounds, such as nitric oxide, are emitted. This seemingly simple and innocuous process turns out to have some vicious side effects. The carbon monoxide emitted from burning of fossil fuels, the automobile in particular, is breathed by people and produces carbon monoxide poisoning. Carbon dioxide is emitted into the atmosphere where it accumulates and produces a possible direct effect on global climate. The nitric oxide is oxidized slowly by oxygen and ozone in the air to form nitrogen dioxide. But the nitrogen dioxide molecules of the air interact with the unburnt hydrocarbons, emitted with automobile exhaust, to produce complex compounds through photochemical reactions in sunlight, giving us the properties of urban smog which cause physical discomfort and harm.

Because of the great importance of automobiles in modern life and because smog is now an almost constant companion of urban populations, it seems wise to take a paragraph or two to describe the chemical events which result from automobile emissions in the atmosphere. Smog is a word which was coined originally to describe the combination of smoke and fog, so characteristic of polluted London air a few decades ago. During the 1940s when the air pollution of Los Angeles, California, became a clearly recognized problem the word was appropriated for what turned out to be a completely different type of air pollution, i.e., a photochemical smog which is identified today with most major metropolitan areas. Photochemical smog is characterized by a relatively high level of oxidants, such as oxygen and ozone. A concentration of more than 0.15 ppm of oxidant for 1 h is considered a serious photochemical smog. It is interesting to note that Los Angeles experienced 29% days of smog above the 0.15 ppm oxidant level during 1964 and 1965, while most cities had less than 5%.

The hydrocarbons emitted in automobile exhaust play a very complex role in the formation of photochemical smog. The whole complex chemical process begins when nitrogen dioxide formed in automobile exhaust is broken down photochemically by ultraviolet light from the sun to form nitric oxide and atomic oxygen. The sequence of reactions which follows this are shown in Table 14, and these will now be explained in sequence. The atomic oxygen is now combined with molecular oxygen in the air to form ozone, which itself is a strong

table 14
reaction schemes for photochemical smog

1. $NO_2 + light \longrightarrow NO + O$
2. $O + O_2 \longrightarrow O_3$
3. $O_3 + NO \longrightarrow NO_2 + O_2$
4. $O + H_c \longrightarrow H_cO^*$
5. $H_cO^* + O_2 \longrightarrow H_cO_3^*$
6. $H_cO_3^* + H_c \longrightarrow$ Aldehydes, ketones, etc.
7. $H_cO_3^* + NO \longrightarrow H_cO_2^* + NO_2$
8. $H_cO_3^* + O_2 \longrightarrow O_3 + H_3O_2^*$
9. $H_cO_x^* + NO_2 \longrightarrow$ Peroxyacyl nitrates

Source: Modified from "Cleaning Our Environment, The Chemical Basis for Action," American Chemical Society, Washington, D.C., 1969, p. 38.

oxidant. In step 3 the ozone oxidizes nitric oxide to form nitrogen dioxide and molecular oxygen. In the fourth process listed, atomic oxygen combines with a hydrocarbon H_c to form a chemical radical H_cO^*. A chemical radical such as this is involved in a series of reactions resulting in the formation of other radicals which react with molecular oxygen, hydrocarbons, and nitric oxide as shown in lines 5, 6, and 7. The products of these reactions are $H_cO_3^*$, aldehydes, ketones, $H_cO_2^*$, and NO_2. The formaldehydes and aldehydes in the polluted air cause the irritation of the eyes one experiences from smog. Other reactions are shown in lines 8 and 9, in which the $H_cO_3^*$ radical reacts with molecular oxygen to form more ozone and $H_cO_2^*$, while there are further reactions between hydrocarbon radicals and NO_2 to yield peroxyacyl nitrates known as PAN.

It is known that the presence of PAN in air around plants caused an abrupt decrease in photosynthesis. It causes plant damage only when light is present. But PAN itself is generated as a result of the lengthy series of chemical events shown in Table 14 of which the first reaction is photochemical requiring the presence of light. Photosynthesis itself requires light, so the two events coincide in activity during daylight hours to result in a reduction of photosynthesis. We should remind ourselves that photosynthesis is the cornerstone of all life on earth. Photosynthesizing plants are the beginning of the entire food chain, of the whole complex web of life, and it is also the only principal source of oxygen in the air. Damage plants and one is literally strangling life itself. Ironically most agricultural plants, upon which we depend for food, are more sensitive to air pollution than are other plants. The oxidants in photochemical smog, particularly ozone, cause serious plant damage through oxidation of chloroplasts, mitochondrial membranes, enzymes, and growth factors.

The enormous quantities of nitrogen and sulfur sent into the air fall out and wash out over the earth's land and ocean surface. The nitrogen cycle and the sulfur cycle between soil and plants are essential to all life. The great concern we have today is: Exactly what is happening to these life-giving cycles as man dumps great amounts of nitrogen and sulfur into the atmosphere? We know that rainfall absorbs these substances and becomes more acidic. We know that the chemical character of some bodies of water is being changed, but what about the soil surfaces of the world? If a few species of soil bacteria were destroyed because of chemical imbalance, all life itself would grind to a halt. For it is these soil bacteria which engage in nitrogen fixation, and they provide plants with the nitrogen required to form the amino acids which are basic ingredients of proteins. Nitrogen is continually entering the air from the breakdown of decaying organic matter through the action of denitrifying bacteria. Destroy these bacteria and the nitrogen cycle is broken. Destroy the nitrogen-fixing bacteria and the cycle is again broken. The most critical problem, in terms of the future of life on earth, pivots about the question: Precisely what is happening to these biochemical cycles upon which all life is so inexorably dependent? The unfortunate fact is that we really do not know. We know only that very serious disruption of the biochemical cycles could spell disaster.

conclusions

Man's concern with knowledge about weather and climate must continue to advance for a long time into the future. The physical mechanisms which drive the weather systems of the world must be understood in order that we can predict future trends of climate for various regions of the world, as well as the global climate of the earth. Our present state of knowledge concerning physiological responses of organisms to climate is very meager and must be substantially improved if man is to appreciate the consequences of climate change on living systems. The interaction of climate and organisms is that body of knowledge known as ecology. It is this duality of the abiotic and biotic components of the world in which we live which makes the subject of ecology both challenging and fascinating. Man is now beginning to realize that he must have an ecological conscience and must understand precisely how it is that ecosystems function in order to maintain a healthy world.

Man produces climate changes with nearly everything he does, whether he is clearing a field, building a house, paving a highway or airfield, or polluting the atmosphere. In earlier times inadvertent modification of climate was more limited than it is today, although slash-and-burn agricultural practices have certainly caused smoke in the sky for thousands of years. Today the world is crowded with people, the productive lands are occupied with agriculture, and urban areas represent massive accretion of people, industries, and means of transportation. Although the world can carry more people than it does today, there is little doubt that the management cost for doing so increases enormously, and the quality of life for the people of the future will degenerate. Zero population-growth rate must be achieved as soon as possible, and the earlier it is accomplished, the better will be the future for mankind. More people require more food, which in turn requires more fertilizers on farms and fields. More power is consumed with production of crops, supply of fertilizer, and delivery of food to the table. The entire process of food production creates serious side effects for a crowded planet, less space for recreation, and more pollution of air and water. The machinery which is necessary to deliver the fertilizers, harvest the crops, and distribute and store food implies further depletion of resources, increased expenditures of energy, and massive potential pollution. Demand for more products by a growing world population will produce increased pollution and other environmental stress. Global climate changes could be a consequence of massive atmospheric inputs, and, if this does occur during the generations to come, man will be challenged to correct it and to keep the world productive.

Whether or not the global climate is changing at the present time, as a result of input of carbon dioxide or of aerosols and dust, we do now know for certain. We believe indeed it might be, and in fact we feel certain the global climate must be changing, but to date scientists have been unable to prove cause and effect concerning climate change. A change of climate for any region of the world is likely to portend serious consequences with respect to the manner of life for the people of the region, particularly as it relates to their agricultural practices. We have seen how insects, viruses, fungi, bacteria, and other pathogens respond to climatic events and how entire crops are devastated as the result of the weather and climate of a region. We have learned how insects and pathogens are carried by the wind across thousands of miles of land or sea. If climate conditions are favorable for the development of an organism, throughout the critical stages of its life history, then the consequences for the prey, whether animal or plant, can be very serious. Understanding the complex interactions of climate and communities of organisms is extremely difficult, but these things must be understood if man is going to assume his ever-increasing responsibility for cultivating and managing the landscapes of the world. As the planet becomes more and more crowded with human population, all the ingenuity, skill, and knowledge man can muster must be used for his management of the earth's ecosystems, in order to avoid pandemics of disease, famine through crop failure, catastrophic climate change, resource depletion, and social breakdown. At center stage for the beginning of the next act is the status of our knowledge concerning climate and life and our ability to respond to changing events in a sensible, rational manner.

index

73 74   7 6 5 4 3 2